T0113916

Word of the Day

from the Book of Romans

Sherol L. Southerland

WestBow Press books may be ordered through booksellers or by contacting:

WestBow Press
A Division of Thomas Nelson & Zondervan
1663 Liberty Drive
Bloomington, IN 47403
www.westbowpress.com
844-714-3454

ISBN: 978-1-6642-4879-3 (sc)
ISBN: 978-1-6642-4880-9 (hc)
ISBN: 978-1-6642-4878-6 (e)

Library of Congress Control Number: 2021950003

Print information available on the last page.

WestBow Press rev. date: 11/05/2021

Acknowledgments

Kenneth, LeCora, Kenzi, and Brendan: You are my gifts from God and my inspiration. I am honored to be your mother and "Grandme", and I endeavor to live my life as an example for you to follow.

The WOTD Group: Thank you for rockin' with me for the past seven years. God continues to show His faithfulness to us and we continue to grow in number and faith. Tamika, Talaya, Alfreda, Barbara, and LaShawn, thank you for willingly standing in the gap when I need you.

From the Author

This second installment in the *Word of the Day* devotional series has been a long time coming. My journey through the book of Romans was transformational for my Christian walk. I was encouraged, affirmed, empowered, convicted, and had to repent. I have come to understand and appreciate God's grace and mercy even more. I have come to understand and appreciate what Jesus's death and resurrection mean for me (and you) even more. I am even more excited about God's love for humanity and the benefits of being a child of God. I am even more confident about who I am in Christ. I believe even more that ABSOLUTELY EVERYTHING I go through will work out for my good in the end. I am more determined to tell others about what salvation is and why we all need it. I have an even greater understanding of God's standard of living for those of us who call Him Father, and why it is so important that we don't live as the world lives. I am even more determined to stand for Christ no matter who or what it costs me.

Whereas the first devotional represented me stepping out in faith despite fear, *Word of the Day from the Book of Romans* represents my determination to use what God has gifted and instructed me to do no matter what obstacles present themselves. This work has been a press amid transitions and challenges in my life; AND, God has been faithful. I have been pruned and have had to sacrifice; AND, God has been faithful. I am so glad that this second installment in the *Word of the Day* devotional series is finished, and now in your hands. I hope that you will open yourself up to being transformed as you invest in your spiritual growth by spending time with God in His word. The Holy Spirit may have you progress through a different devotion each day or sit with one for several days or weeks. Sit with each devotion and chew on this spiritual nutrition until you get all the nutrients that God wants you to get out of it.

I love you in the Lord!

Rev. Sherol

day 1

Romans 1:2-4: ***"God promised this Good News long ago through his prophets in the Holy Scriptures. The Good News is about his Son. In his earthly life, he was born into King David's family line, and he was shown to be the Son of God when he was raised from the dead by the power of the Holy Spirit. He is Jesus Christ our Lord."***

Jesus Christ, the living Lord and Savior, reconciles lost humanity to a holy God. That's Good News! Jesus paid the ultimate price - death - for our sins so that our relationship with God could be restored. That's Good News! Those who believe in and accept Jesus as Lord and Savior are forgiven and restored. That's Good News! God's free gift of salvation through Jesus Christ to all who believe and accept Jesus as Lord and Savior is Good News! Jesus Christ is coming back again to receive to Himself those who belong to Him. That is Good News! The Kingdom of God is at hand. That is Good News! It's too good to keep to yourself; so, tell somebody who needs to know God's love for them through the saving power of Jesus Christ, our Lord!

Personal Reflection/Application/Prayer: How has God spoken to you through today's WOTD as it relates to your life? How does today's WOTD speak to you/your situation? What was affirmed? For what do you need to repent? What will you do differently going forward? What commitment to your spiritual growth are you going to make? Is there something that you need from God in order to live His word daily? If not for yourself, for whom do you need to pray as it relates to this WOTD? What can you thank God for and/or declare in confidence according to God's word? What can you boldly and confidently ask God for according to His word? Use the space below to record your personal revelation from God about how these verses apply to you and/or write a personal prayer to God.

day 2

Romans 1:16-17: ***"For I am not ashamed of this Good News about Christ. It is the power of God at work, saving everyone who believes—the Jew first and also the Gentile. This Good News tells us how God makes us right in his sight. This is accomplished from start to finish by faith. As the Scriptures say, 'It is through faith that a righteous person has life.'"***

Have you ever heard anyone say things like, "I have to get myself together before I go to church" or say things like "I'm a good person and I help people" during conversations about salvation? Sadly, many people believe the devil's lie that they can get themselves "together" (whatever that looks like). Equally as sad is that there are people who believe that doing good things makes them right with God. There are two very clear problems with these two lines of thought that these verses address: (1) None of us can get ourselves together by ourselves. Only the power of God can do that and He does it through Jesus Christ. (2) Being a good person and doing good things can never make us right with God. Only faith in Jesus Christ can make us right with God. Isn't it good news to know that it isn't your responsibility, with your faulty self, to fix yourself or earn salvation?! The Good News is that God gave that responsibility to Jesus, who is without fault, and he fulfilled that responsibility; all you have to do is believe in him! The next time that you are in a conversation with someone who says that they have to get themselves together or who feels that their good deeds are enough to get them into heaven, share the Good News of these verses with them. Give them the truth in the face of the devil's lies. You could win a soul for the Kingdom.

Personal Reflection/Application/Prayer: How has God spoken to you through today's WOTD as it relates to your life? How does today's WOTD speak to you/your situation? What was affirmed? For what do you need to repent? What will you do differently going forward? What commitment to your spiritual growth are you going to make? Is there something that you need from God in order to live His word daily? If not for yourself, for whom do you need to pray as it relates to this

WOTD? What can you thank God for and/or declare in confidence according to God's word? What can you boldly and confidently ask God for according to His word? Use the space below to record your personal revelation from God about how these verses apply to you and/or write a personal prayer to God.

day 3

Romans 1:18-20: ***"But God shows his anger from heaven against all sinful, wicked people who suppress the truth by their wickedness. They know the truth about God because he has made it obvious to them. For ever since the world was created, people have seen the earth and sky. Through everything God made, they can clearly see his invisible qualities—his eternal power and divine nature. So they have no excuse for not knowing God."***

Sinful behavior/wickedness is all around us - from being conscious, overt, and blatant to being unconscious, subtle, and hidden. In the same way, the truth about God is all around us; He reveals himself to us through everything He made. Sin is universal and no one is above sinning; yet, we have a choice in how we respond to its temptation: surrender to the One, True, Living God in faith and turn from wickedness or suppress the truth by our sinful, wicked behavior. Whatever we choose, we have no excuse for not knowing God. As you go through today, consider and even write down how God reveals His eternal power and divine nature through creation, including you. Then, confess those attributes to Him as an act of worship.

Personal Reflection/Application/Prayer: How has God spoken to you through today's WOTD as it relates to your life? How does today's WOTD speak to you/ your situation? What was affirmed? For what do you need to repent? What will you do differently going forward? What commitment to your spiritual growth are you going to make? Is there something that you need from God in order to live His word daily? If not for yourself, for whom do you need to pray as it relates to this WOTD? What can you thank God for and/or declare in confidence according to God's word? What can you boldly and confidently ask God for according to His word? Use the space below to record your personal revelation from God about how these verses apply to you and/or write a personal prayer to God.

Romans 1:21-23: ***"Yes, they knew God, but they wouldn't worship him as God or even give him thanks. And they began to think up foolish ideas of what God was like. As a result, their minds became dark and confused. Claiming to be wise, they instead became utter fools. And instead of worshiping the glorious, ever-living God, they worshiped idols made to look like mere people and birds and animals and reptiles."***

What we learn about God through observing creation isn't all there is to know about God. While God's creation is marvelous and amazing, showing His eternal power and divine nature as Creator, God's creation is never to be worshiped - neither things nor people. To do so is idolatrous, wicked, and foolish. Creation cannot tell you how to live for God. Don't allow your self-proclaimed wisdom about what you think you know about God to lead you down a path of idol worship in any form. Only through seeking an intimate relationship with the One, True, Living God, putting Him above everything and everyone else in our lives daily (i.e., worship), do we truly learn who God is and how He wants us to live.

Personal Reflection/Application/Prayer: How has God spoken to you through today's WOTD as it relates to your life? How does today's WOTD speak to you/ your situation? What was affirmed? For what do you need to repent? What will you do differently going forward? What commitment to your spiritual growth are you going to make? Is there something that you need from God in order to live His word daily? If not for yourself, for whom do you need to pray as it relates to this WOTD? What can you thank God for and/or declare in confidence according to God's word? What can you boldly and confidently ask God for according to His word? Use the space below to record your personal revelation from God about how these verses apply to you and/or write a personal prayer to God.

day 5

Romans 1:24-25: ***"So God abandoned them to do whatever shameful things their hearts desired. As a result, they did vile and degrading things with each other's bodies. They traded the truth about God for a lie. So they worshiped and served the things God created instead of the Creator himself, who is worthy of eternal praise! Amen."***

How can God, who is good, gracious, merciful, loving, and forgiving "abandon" people when His word says that He will never leave nor forsake us[1]? Is this a contradiction in the Bible? Absolutely not. God is all of these things and more. God is a patient God, more patient with us than we are with other people or even ourselves. God is holy and just and He cannot lie. God makes it clear that there are consequences for sin and there comes a point in all of our lives where we will experience the consequences of our sin - both natural and spiritual consequences - if we refuse to worship the One, True, Living God. Here "abandoned" means that God gave the people over to themselves - to their fleshly desires - because they refused to worship Him. It is a dangerous thing to be "abandoned" by God. When God abandons, there is no barrier/filter/protective covering. You are exposed, meaning that it is open season for the devil to have his way, infiltrating and consuming the minds and hearts of people so that they will do whatever whenever. People live with a truly "It's whatever" mindset and their actions show it. I don't know about you; but, I don't ever want God to give me over to myself. I will worship Him and Him alone no matter who else chooses or refuses to do so.

Personal Reflection/Application/Prayer: How has God spoken to you through today's WOTD as it relates to your life? How does today's WOTD speak to you/ your situation? What was affirmed? For what do you need to repent? What will you do differently going forward? What commitment to your spiritual growth are you going to make? Is there something that you need from God in order to live His word daily? If not for yourself, for whom do you need to pray as it relates to this

[1] Deuteronomy 31:6

WOTD? What can you thank God for and/or declare in confidence according to God's word? What can you boldly and confidently ask God for according to His word? Use the space below to record your personal revelation from God about how these verses apply to you and/or write a personal prayer to God.

Romans 1:26-27: ***"That is why God abandoned them to their shameful desires. Even the women turned against the natural way to have sex and instead indulged in sex with each other. And the men, instead of having normal sexual relations with women, burned with lust for each other. Men did shameful things with other men, and as a result of this sin, they suffered within themselves the penalty they deserved."***

God created the natural way for sexual intimacy to occur and any other way is unnatural, perverse, and an abomination. Even though these verses speak specifically about homosexuality, ALL sexual sin (i.e., fornication, adultery, masturbation, pornography, etc…) is sin against one's own body[2] and harms us physically, mentally, emotionally, and spiritually. Spiritually speaking, our bodies are not our own.[3] God bought our bodies at the price of His Son's death. Our body is the place where God deposits His Spirit once we accept Jesus as our Lord and Savior and it must be honored at all times.[4] To persist in this sin after God has warned and instructed you to stop, repent, and live righteously, results in spiritual death. You may be physically alive, but you are spiritually DEAD. Ask yourself: Is the temporary satisfaction that sexual sin gives worth God abandoning me to my shameful ways – to be devoured by the devil (who, by the way, is watching and waiting for this to happen)? Is it worth my spiritual death and separation from God? If today's WOTD applies to you in this area, know that this is yet another warning and instruction straight from the word of God to stop persisting in sexual sin. Neither your rationalizations and justifications nor the world's approval can stand against God's word. No one or thing is more important than your relationship and fellowship with God. To value someone or thing more is to be idolatrous. Nothing is worth God withdrawing His hand from over your life. Honor your body as an act of worship unto God every day.

---

[2] 1 Corinthians 6:18

[3] 1 Corinthians 6:19-20

[4] 1 Corinthians 1:22; Ephesians 1:13-14

Personal Reflection/Application/Prayer: How has God spoken to you through today's WOTD as it relates to your life? How does today's WOTD speak to you/ your situation? What was affirmed? For what do you need to repent? What will you do differently going forward? What commitment to your spiritual growth are you going to make? Is there something that you need from God in order to live His word daily? If not for yourself, for whom do you need to pray as it relates to this WOTD? What can you thank God for and/or declare in confidence according to God's word? What can you boldly and confidently ask God for according to His word? Use the space below to record your personal revelation from God about how these verses apply to you and/or write a personal prayer to God.

day 7

Romans 1:28-31: "***Since they thought it foolish to acknowledge God, he abandoned them to their foolish thinking and let them do things that should never be done. Their lives became full of every kind of wickedness, sin, greed, hate, envy, murder, quarreling, deception, malicious behavior, and gossip. They are backstabbers, haters of God, insolent [boldly rude or disrespectful], proud, and boastful. They invent new ways of sinning, and they disobey their parents. They refuse to understand, break their promises, are heartless, and have no mercy."*** While not an exhaustive list of sins, these verses let us know that sin comes in many forms. The shift in verb tense from past to present (e.g., "their lives became...They are…") lets us know that the same sins that were committed in Bible times are still being committed today, along with new ones. Any way you slice it, rejecting God, His will and His way, is wicked; refusing to worship God alone is wicked; putting anyone or anything above God (in your actions even if not in your words) is wicked; refusing to obey God in any way, shape, form, or fashion = wickedness = sin. Stop at this moment; HUMBLE yourself and pray: for yourself first, for those whom you know, and those whom you don't know. Ask God to search you/them and to take out anything that should not be at its root as He finds it. Ask God to create a clean heart within you and renew a right spirit within you.[5] REPENT for your sins and pray for repentance across our nation, SEEK God's face; TURN FROM your wicked ways; WORSHIP the One True Living God. God is faithful to forgive you and He will give you a new beginning.

Personal Reflection/Application/Prayer: How has God spoken to you through today's WOTD as it relates to your life? How does today's WOTD speak to you/ your situation? What was affirmed? For what do you need to repent? What will you do differently going forward? What commitment to your spiritual growth are you going to make? Is there something that you need from God in order to live His word daily? If not for yourself, for whom do you need to pray

[5] Psalm 51:10

as it relates to this WOTD? What can you thank God for and/or declare in confidence according to God's word? What can you boldly and confidently ask God for according to His word? Use the space below to record your personal revelation from God about how these verses apply to you and/or write a personal prayer to God.

Romans 1:32: ***"They know God's justice requires that those who do these things deserve to die, yet they do them anyway. Worse yet, they encourage others to do them, too."*** According to this verse, there is something worse than sinning: encouraging others to sin. The Bible is full of scriptures about the consequences of influencing/leading others to sin. Real talk: Anyone who truly loves and respects you, loves and respects God, and has your best interests at heart will not encourage you to disobey God; especially, if they know the consequences of sin. Equally so, if you truly love and respect yourself, love and respect those in your circle of influence and have their best interests at heart, you will not encourage them to disobey God. If you're honest with yourself, you have to admit that you have been on both sides of this equation at some point in your life whether you realized it or not and whether or not you fully understood the consequences of your actions. This may even be where you are as you read this WOTD. Glory be to God that you don't have to continue in this way. Perhaps, you've repented for your sins but never repented for encouraging other people to sin. If God's grace and mercy are enabling you to be alive at this moment to read and understand His word, as well as the consequences for your obedience and disobedience, God is giving you a chance to repent not only for sinning against Him yourself but also for encouraging others to sin, which carries heavy repercussions. Because of Jesus, you can be forgiven. Because of Jesus, the curse of sinful behavior - even generational - can be broken today. Because of Jesus, your slate can be wiped clean. Because of Jesus, you can be restored and what you've lost as a result of sin can be restored to you. Choose repentance and restoration today.

Personal Reflection/Application/Prayer: How has God spoken to you through today's WOTD as it relates to your life? How does today's WOTD speak to you/ your situation? What was affirmed? For what do you need to repent? What will you do differently going forward? What commitment to your spiritual growth are you going to make? Is there something that you need from God in order to live His word daily? If not for yourself, for whom do you need to pray as it relates to this WOTD? What can you thank God for and/or declare in

confidence according to God's word? What can you boldly and confidently ask God for according to His word? Use the space below to record your personal revelation from God about how these verses apply to you and/or write a personal prayer to God.

day 9

Romans 2:1: ***"You may think you can condemn such people, but you are just as bad, and you have no excuse! When you say they are wicked and should be punished, you are condemning yourself, for you who judge others do these very same things."*** The hypocritical Jews believed and acted as if they were superior to the Gentiles and condemned the Gentiles for their wicked, sinful behavior even though they were doing the same things. The Jews knew better than to engage in such wicked behavior because they were God's people. God is a just God; He is sovereign and only God can pronounce a final judgment over a person's life. Sin is sin and every person, no matter who we are or what we have, will stand before God and be judged for our behavior. If you are a child of God, your life should be an example for others to follow; you should be light in darkness so that others can see how to live. Take a moment for self-reflection and introspection: Do you qualify your sinful behavior as if it isn't as bad as someone else's? Have you told yourself and others, "It's not that serious" when your sinfulness is under the microscope to minimize your rebellion against God? Is there a part of you that thinks you are better than others who sin? If you answered "Yes" to any of these questions, remember: Judgment starts with God's people.[6] Hypocrisy doesn't look good on a child of God and it is actually a slap in the face to God. So, trade it in for humility and transparency before God and people. Get your house in order and live as a child of the light.

Personal Reflection/Application/Prayer: How has God spoken to you through today's WOTD as it relates to your life? How does today's WOTD speak to you/ your situation? What was affirmed? For what do you need to repent? What will you do differently going forward? What commitment to your spiritual growth are you going to make? Is there something that you need from God in order to live His word daily? If not for yourself, for whom do you need to pray as it relates to this WOTD? What can you thank God for and/or declare in

[6] 1 Peter 4:17

confidence according to God's word? What can you boldly and confidently ask God for according to His word? Use the space below to record your personal revelation from God about how these verses apply to you and/or write a personal prayer to God.

day 10

Romans 2:2-3: ***"And we know that God, in his justice, will punish anyone who does such things. Since you judge others for doing these things, why do you think you can avoid God's judgment when you do the same things?"*** Hopefully, you value your relationship with God enough to wrestle with the hard questions about yourself and your actions. Yesterday, you were asked to take a moment for self-reflection and introspection and to answer three "yes or no" questions. Hopefully, you were honest with yourself and God. The question in today's WOTD goes beyond your "yes" or "no" and gets at the root of hypocrisy. I encourage you to wrestle with it and give yourself and God an honest answer. God already knows. Let your honesty and transparency lead you to repentance, which opens the door for your deliverance and transformation.

Personal Reflection/Application/Prayer: How has God spoken to you through today's WOTD as it relates to your life? How does today's WOTD speak to you/ your situation? What was affirmed? For what do you need to repent? What will you do differently going forward? What commitment to your spiritual growth are you going to make? Is there something that you need from God in order to live His word daily? If not for yourself, for whom do you need to pray as it relates to this WOTD? What can you thank God for and/or declare in confidence according to God's word? What can you boldly and confidently ask God for according to His word? Use the space below to record your personal revelation from God about how these verses apply to you and/or write a personal prayer to God.

day 11

Romans 2:4-5: ***"Don't you see how wonderfully, kind, tolerant, and patient God is with you? Does this mean nothing to you? Can't you see that his kindness is intended to turn you from your sin? But because you are stubborn and refuse to turn from your sin, you are storing up terrible punishment for yourself. For a day of anger is coming, when God's righteous judgment will be revealed."*** ~ "I owe you a whippin'," which my mother used to say to us, came to mind as I read these verses. Sometimes, instead of giving us a whippin' for being hard-headed, my mother would fuss and end with "A hard head makes a soft tail." The next time that we were hard-headed, she'd say, "I already owe you a whippin'." Not realizing that Ma was extending grace and mercy, we would inevitably cross the line and she would give us justice: all of what she "owed" us for our disobedience. The storehouse of whippin' could contain no more and the rod of discipline was no longer spared. We could never say that we didn't know or understand why we were being disciplined because she told us while she was whippin' us. Whether after fussin' or whippin', Ma would always say, "If I didn't love you, I wouldn't care." You may have a similar story. While I didn't realize it then, my mother exemplified the wonderful, kind, tolerant, and patient parent that God is to us. She also demonstrated the revelation of righteous judgment when she needed to. Sadly, we often misinterpret the intent behind God's kindness, tolerance, and patience with us as permission to continue in our sin. God is more patient with us than we deserve; yet, He is so because He loves us so. He gives us opportunity after opportunity to turn from our sinful ways. He warns us, letting us know that our stubbornness and refusal to be obedient is making our bed hard and we will have to lie in it. "...you are storing up terrible punishment for yourself" = "I owe you a whippin'." The day is going to come when God's storehouse of whippin' will contain no more and His righteous judgment WILL be revealed. Whether we are saved or unsaved, we are accountable to God for our sins. Are you prepared to receive what you have stored up for yourself? God's grace and mercy over your life - His wonderful kindness, tolerance, and patience - should never be taken for granted. Jesus' death on the cross for our sins should never be minimized or dismissed.

Let nothing hinder your relationship - worship - fellowship. Choose at this moment to repent and turn from whatever sins you need to turn from. God is faithful to forgive you and cleanse you from all unrighteousness through the blood of Jesus.[7] Thank Him for it!

Personal Reflection/Application/Prayer: How has God spoken to you through today's WOTD as it relates to your life? How does today's WOTD speak to you/your situation? What was affirmed? For what do you need to repent? What will you do differently going forward? What commitment to your spiritual growth are you going to make? Is there something that you need from God in order to live His word daily? If not for yourself, for whom do you need to pray as it relates to this WOTD? What can you thank God for and/or declare in confidence according to God's word? What can you boldly and confidently ask God for according to His word? Use the space below to record your personal revelation from God about how these verses apply to you and/or write a personal prayer to God.

---

[7] 1 John 1:9

day 12

Romans 2:6-8: **"He will judge everyone according to what they have done. He will give eternal life to those who keep on doing good, seeking after the glory and honor and immortality that God offers. But he will pour out his anger and wrath on those who live for themselves, who refuse to obey the truth and instead live lives of wickedness."** While we can never earn salvation by doing good deeds, ALL of us will be judged by our deeds - whether we lived for God or ourselves. Living for God = doing good = judgment: receiving eternal life. Living for ourselves = wickedness = judgment: receiving God's wrath and anger. The good news is that you get to choose, and the first choice is whether to accept Jesus Christ as your Lord and Savior. The second choice is whether to submit to Jesus' lordship over your life and live to glorify God rather than yourself. You see, no one can condemn you; but, you can condemn yourself by how you live. Choose to live a life of faithful obedience to the One and only faithful God with the peace of knowing that eternal life is your reward.

Personal Reflection/Application/Prayer: How has God spoken to you through today's WOTD as it relates to your life? How does today's WOTD speak to you/your situation? What was affirmed? For what do you need to repent? What will you do differently going forward? What commitment to your spiritual growth are you going to make? Is there something that you need from God in order to live His word daily? If not for yourself, for whom do you need to pray as it relates to this WOTD? What can you thank God for and/or declare in confidence according to God's word? What can you boldly and confidently ask God for according to His word? Use the space below to record your personal revelation from God about how these verses apply to you and/or write a personal prayer to God.

day 13

Romans 2:9-11: ***"There will be trouble and calamity for everyone who keeps on doing what is evil—for the Jew first and also for the Gentile. But there will be glory and honor and peace from God for all who do good—for the Jew first and also for the Gentile. For God shows no favoritism."*** God shows no bias when He judges and all of humanity will be judged when we stand before Him on Judgment Day. We cannot earn salvation; however, doing good deeds (i.e., doing what pleases God) is our response of gratitude for what God did for us by sending His Son, Jesus Christ, to die on the cross for our sins so that we can receive His free gift of salvation. Determine to show our Lord and Savior every day how much you appreciate Him for dying in your place so that you could receive salvation and be restored to a right relationship with God.

Personal Reflection/Application/Prayer: How has God spoken to you through today's WOTD as it relates to your life? How does today's WOTD speak to you/your situation? What was affirmed? For what do you need to repent? What will you do differently going forward? What commitment to your spiritual growth are you going to make? Is there something that you need from God in order to live His word daily? If not for yourself, for whom do you need to pray as it relates to this WOTD? What can you thank God for and/or declare in confidence according to God's word? What can you boldly and confidently ask God for according to His word? Use the space below to record your personal revelation from God about how these verses apply to you and/or write a personal prayer to God.

day 14

Romans 2:16: ***"And this is the message I proclaim—that the day is coming when God, through Christ Jesus, will judge everyone's secret life."*** What others don't know in secret, God knows. What others don't see in secret, God sees. What others don't hear in secret, God hears. To know right from wrong and choose to continue doing wrong, even in secret, will not go unjudged. The day is coming when God, through Christ Jesus, will judge your secret life. When you stand before God the Judge in the Courts of Heaven, what judgment will He render in your case? Will you be found guilty and condemned for what you did in secret or will you receive glory, honor, and peace from God[8]? Today is the day and now is the time to get right with God.

Personal Reflection/Application/Prayer: How has God spoken to you through today's WOTD as it relates to your life? How does today's WOTD speak to you/ your situation? What was affirmed? For what do you need to repent? What will you do differently going forward? What commitment to your spiritual growth are you going to make? Is there something that you need from God in order to live His word daily? If not for yourself, for whom do you need to pray as it relates to this WOTD? What can you thank God for and/or declare in confidence according to God's word? What can you boldly and confidently ask God for according to His word? Use the space below to record your personal revelation from God about how these verses apply to you and/or write a personal prayer to God.

[8] Romans 2:10

day 15

Romans 2: 21-23: ***"Well then, if you teach others, why don't you teach yourself? You tell others not to steal, but do you steal? You say it is wrong to commit adultery, but do you commit adultery? You condemn idolatry, but do you use items stolen from pagan temples? You are so proud of knowing the law, but you dishonor God by breaking it."*** Here, Paul calls out the Jews who criticized others for breaking God's law while excusing themselves for doing the same. God's word gives us the guidelines/principles by which we are to live our lives. Before we attempt to use God's word to point out someone else's wrong, each of us needs to screen our own lives against God's word first to see where we are and are NOT pleasing God. As the Holy Spirit reveals our sinfulness, we need to be quick to repent; ask God's forgiveness; and live God's word. Otherwise, we are hypocrites - plain and simple - and living a hypocritical life is never pleasing to God. It makes a mockery of God and God will not be mocked; whatever we sow, we will reap.[9] If you truly value your relationship with God, pray and ask Him to search you and reveal to you those things about you that are displeasing to Him. Because He loves you, He will. AS (not IF) He reveals them to you, show your love for Him by being quick to repent of your sins; ask Him to forgive you. Because He loves you, He will. Then, commit to living a life that shows that you are His. If you love Him, you will.

Personal Reflection/Application/Prayer: How has God spoken to you through today's WOTD as it relates to your life? How does today's WOTD speak to you/ your situation? What was affirmed? For what do you need to repent? What will you do differently going forward? What commitment to your spiritual growth are you going to make? Is there something that you need from God in order to live His word daily? If not for yourself, for whom do you need to pray as it relates to this WOTD? What can you thank God for and/or declare in confidence according to God's word? What can you boldly and confidently ask God for according to His word? Use the space below to record your personal revelation from God about how these verses apply to you and/or write a personal prayer to God.

[9] Galatians 6:7-8

day 16

Romans 2:29: ***"No, a true Jew is one whose heart is right with God. And true circumcision is not merely obeying the letter of the law; rather, it is a change of heart produced by the Spirit. And a person with a changed heart seeks praise from God, not people."*** Physical circumcision was performed in OT times as a requirement and sign of covenant relationship with God. Both Jesus and Paul criticized the Jews because their hearts were far from God even though they were physically circumcised as religious law required. As this verse teaches, true circumcision isn't just a physical act; it is a spiritual one. True circumcision is a change of one's heart; that is, a heart that has been made right with God through the Holy Spirit. A person who has been truly circumcised seeks praises from God, not people. At the end of the day, God is less concerned with you following the routines and rituals of religion than He is with the condition of your heart towards Him, which will determine how you live your life. After all, a person can follow the routines and rituals of religion and still have a hard heart towards God and others. Questions: What is the condition of your heart? Are you truly circumcised? If your answer is "No", what is keeping you from giving your heart to God? Why haven't you yielded to the Holy Spirit's work in your life?

Personal Reflection/Application/Prayer: How has God spoken to you through today's WOTD as it relates to your life? How does today's WOTD speak to you/your situation? What was affirmed? For what do you need to repent? What will you do differently going forward? What commitment to your spiritual growth are you going to make? Is there something that you need from God in order to live His word daily? If not for yourself, for whom do you need to pray as it relates to this WOTD? What can you thank God for and/or declare in confidence according to God's word? What can you boldly and confidently ask God for according to His word? Use the space below to record your personal revelation from God about how these verses apply to you and/or write a personal prayer to God.

day 17

Romans 3:3-4: ***"True, some of them [Jews] were unfaithful; but just because they were unfaithful, does that mean that God will be unfaithful? Of course not! Even if everyone else is a liar, God is true. As the Scriptures say about him, 'You will be proved right in what you say, and you will win your case in court.'"*** God is always true and right. God's word is always true and right. God is faithful to do just what He said He will do. God gives us His word to show us how we are to live. The word of God tells us who God is, who we are (both in and outside of a relationship with Him through Jesus Christ), the depth of our sinfulness and the consequences of sin, the depth of His love for us, and the promises guaranteed when we receive His free gift of salvation to save us from the penalty of our sins. The word of God not only tells us that ALL of us will stand before Him and be judged, it tells us what will happen to us based upon our judgment outcome. Every action spoken in God's word will come to pass. Yet, people choose every day to ignore God and His word and live as if there will be no accountability. No matter who you are or what you believe, the truth is that you are accountable and you will be judged for your actions. No matter who you are or what you believe, God will be proved right when Judgment Day comes.[10] One thing you can be certain of is that there will be no do-over of your case. The next second, minute, hour, day, week, month, or year is not promised to you. All you have is now. What are you going to do with it? When you have to give an account of your life before God, what will your life say on your behalf about what eternity will be for you? What will the truth be about you? Think about these things and get right with God whatever you've got wrong.

Personal Reflection/Application/Prayer: How has God spoken to you through today's WOTD as it relates to your life? How does today's WOTD speak to you/your situation? What was affirmed? For what do you need to repent? What will you do differently going forward? What commitment to your spiritual growth are you going to make? Is there something that you need from God in order to live His word daily? If not for yourself, for whom do you need to pray as it relates to this

[10] Psalm 51:4

WOTD? What can you thank God for and/or declare in confidence according to God's word? What can you boldly and confidently ask God for according to His word? Use the space below to record your personal revelation from God about how these verses apply to you and/or write a personal prayer to God.

day 18

Romans 3:5-9: ***"'But', some might say, 'our sinfulness serves a good purpose, for it helps people see how righteous God is. Isn't it unfair, then, for him to punish us?' (This is merely a human point of view.) Of course not! If God were not entirely fair, how would he be qualified to judge the world? "But", someone might still argue, 'how can God condemn me as a sinner if my dishonesty highlights his truthfulness and brings him more glory?' And some people even slander us by claiming that we say, 'The more we sin, the better it is! Those who say such things deserve to be condemned. Well then, should we conclude that we Jews are better than others? No, not at all, for we have already shown that all people, whether Jew or Gentile, are under the power of sin."*** It amazes me how people, especially those of us who claim to know God, attempt to rationalize and justify our sin. Among the many things that God's word makes clear is that sin is sin no matter who's doing it; no one person's or group of people's sins is acceptable to God; the just penalty for sin is death; every single one of us is powerless in our own right against sin in our lives. If you take time to seriously think about this reality, your individual (and our collective) need for and dependence on the Savior becomes clearer and clearer.

Personal Reflection/Application/Prayer: How has God spoken to you through today's WOTD as it relates to your life? How does today's WOTD speak to you/ your situation? What was affirmed? For what do you need to repent? What will you do differently going forward? What commitment to your spiritual growth are you going to make? Is there something that you need from God in order to live His word daily? If not for yourself, for whom do you need to pray as it relates to this WOTD? What can you thank God for and/or declare in confidence according to God's word? What can you boldly and confidently ask God for according to His word? Use the space below to record your personal revelation from God about how these verses apply to you and/or write a personal prayer to God.

day 19

Romans 3:20-22: ***"For no one can ever be made right with God by doing what the law commands. The law simply shows us how sinful we are. But now God has shown us a way to be made right with him without keeping the requirements of the law, as was promised in the writings of Moses and the prophets long ago. We are made right with God by placing our faith in Jesus Christ. And this is true for everyone who believes, no matter who we are."*** God's law is perfect and not one of us can earn salvation (be made right with God) by keeping the law. God's law does two things for us: reveals God's moral code for our lives and shows us how sinful we are when it comes to living up to that moral code without fail. We can follow the rule of the law and, at the same time, have sin in our hearts and thoughts. Jesus Christ was the only one able to keep God's law perfectly and, no matter who we are, the only way that we can be made right with God is by placing our faith in Jesus Christ. Thank God for sending Jesus to save us and make us right with Him.

Personal Reflection/Application/Prayer: How has God spoken to you through today's WOTD as it relates to your life? How does today's WOTD speak to you/your situation? What was affirmed? For what do you need to repent? What will you do differently going forward? What commitment to your spiritual growth are you going to make? Is there something that you need from God in order to live His word daily? If not for yourself, for whom do you need to pray as it relates to this WOTD? What can you thank God for and/or declare in confidence according to God's word? What can you boldly and confidently ask God for according to His word? Use the space below to record your personal revelation from God about how these verses apply to you and/or write a personal prayer to God.

day 20

Romans 3:23-24: ***"For everyone has sinned; we all fall short of God's glorious standard. Yet God, with undeserved kindness, declares that we are righteous. He did this through Christ Jesus when he freed us from the penalty for our sins."*** None of us has a right to turn our nose up at another person, thinking that we are better than another, because all of us have sinned. None of us can achieve God's high moral standard of living on our own because all of us are slaves to sin and undeserving of being in God's presence. Thanks be to God for looking beyond our faults and seeing our need for salvation. Thanks be to God for sending Jesus Christ to pay the price to free us from the penalty of our sins. Through a relationship with Jesus Christ, we are made right with God. That's a reason to give Him praise!

Personal Reflection/Application/Prayer: How has God spoken to you through today's WOTD as it relates to your life? How does today's WOTD speak to you/your situation? What was affirmed? For what do you need to repent? What will you do differently going forward? What commitment to your spiritual growth are you going to make? Is there something that you need from God in order to live His word daily? If not for yourself, for whom do you need to pray as it relates to this WOTD? What can you thank God for and/or declare in confidence according to God's word? What can you boldly and confidently ask God for according to His word? Use the space below to record your personal revelation from God about how these verses apply to you and/or write a personal prayer to God.

day 21

Romans 3:25: ***"For God presented Jesus as the sacrifice for sin. People are made right with God when they believe that Jesus sacrificed his life, shedding his blood."*** Jesus Christ is THE ONLY way to God. The world offers many different rationalizations and options other than Jesus, including being "spiritual" (which the devil is, by the way) and being a good person/ doing good deeds. Some people even think they have a relationship with God because they pray. Jesus isn't an option; he is THE ONLY option. FAITH (believing in one's heart) IN what JESUS did for humanity - died on the cross to save us from the penalty and power of sin - and accepting Jesus Christ as one's Lord and Savior IS THE ONLY WAY TO BE MADE RIGHT WITH GOD.

Personal Reflection/Application/Prayer: How has God spoken to you through today's WOTD as it relates to your life? How does today's WOTD speak to you/ your situation? What was affirmed? For what do you need to repent? What will you do differently going forward? What commitment to your spiritual growth are you going to make? Is there something that you need from God in order to live His word daily? If not for yourself, for whom do you need to pray as it relates to this WOTD? What can you thank God for and/or declare in confidence according to God's word? What can you boldly and confidently ask God for according to His word? Use the space below to record your personal revelation from God about how these verses apply to you and/or write a personal prayer to God.

day 22

Romans 3:25b-26: ***"This sacrifice shows that God was being fair when he held back and did not punish those who sinned in times past, for he was looking ahead and including them in what he would do in this present time. God did this to demonstrate his righteousness, for he himself is fair and just, and he declares sinners to be right in his sight when they believe in Jesus."*** A pure, unblemished, blood sacrifice was required to atone for sin. Jesus, the only one who was pure and unblemished, the only one who had no sin in him, offered his own life as the blood sacrifice to pay the penalty for the sins of ALL humanity (those who came before him AND those who came after him) for ALL time. Whoever believes this, God declares right in His sight. When we go through the Advent season, anticipating the celebration of the birth of our Lord and Savior Jesus Christ, let us do so with thanksgiving because we know that Jesus was born, lived, and died to make us right with God. Jesus is truly the greatest gift - not under the tree, but on the tree. He died for you and me!

Personal Reflection/Application/Prayer: How has God spoken to you through today's WOTD as it relates to your life? How does today's WOTD speak to you/ your situation? What was affirmed? For what do you need to repent? What will you do differently going forward? What commitment to your spiritual growth are you going to make? Is there something that you need from God in order to live His word daily? If not for yourself, for whom do you need to pray as it relates to this WOTD? What can you thank God for and/or declare in confidence according to God's word? What can you boldly and confidently ask God for according to His word? Use the space below to record your personal revelation from God about how these verses apply to you and/or write a personal prayer to God.

day 23

Romans 3:27-28: ***"Can we boast, then, that we have done anything to be accepted by God? No, because our acquittal is not based on obeying the law. It is based on faith. So we are made right with God through faith and not by obeying the law."*** Not one person can ever truly claim to deserve salvation because of anything we've done. Our sins show us to be undeserving and disqualify us from being in God's presence; our sins make us guilty and deserving of death. The devil keeps a running record of our sins and presents them before God to accuse us of breaking the law.[11] When God looks at those who have placed their faith in Jesus Christ, He sees the shed blood of Jesus covering all of their sins and declares a "Not Guilty" verdict. That is Good News! Thank God for the shed blood of Jesus! Thank God for Jesus' faithfulness in fulfilling the purpose for which God sent Him into this world!

Personal Reflection/Application/Prayer: How has God spoken to you through today's WOTD as it relates to your life? How does today's WOTD speak to you/ your situation? What was affirmed? For what do you need to repent? What will you do differently going forward? What commitment to your spiritual growth are you going to make? Is there something that you need from God in order to live His word daily? If not for yourself, for whom do you need to pray as it relates to this WOTD? What can you thank God for and/or declare in confidence according to God's word? What can you boldly and confidently ask God for according to His word? Use the space below to record your personal revelation from God about how these verses apply to you and/or write a personal prayer to God.

[11] Revelation 12:10

day 24

Romans 3:30-31: **"There is only one God, and he makes people right with himself only by faith, whether they are Jews or Gentiles. Well then, if we emphasize faith, does this mean that we can forget about the law? Of course not! In fact, only when we have faith do we truly fulfill the law."** There are those who believe that the Old Testament is no longer relevant, that it doesn't apply to us because they are "New Testament Christians". Sadly, they have misinterpreted Scripture. Thankfully, we no longer must sacrifice animals on an altar to be forgiven for breaking God's perfect law because Jesus was the ultimate sacrificial lamb, whose blood was shed for the forgiveness of sin for all time. The principles of God's word in the OT are just as relevant today as the principles of God's word in the NT; so, we can never rightfully dismiss either. Jesus is the fulfillment of the OT; Jesus is the One spoken about by the OT prophets who foretold His coming to save us. By putting our faith in Jesus, we can fulfill what the law requires - which is righteousness. Faith in Jesus Christ makes us right with God.

Personal Reflection/Application/Prayer: How has God spoken to you through today's WOTD as it relates to your life? How does today's WOTD speak to you/ your situation? What was affirmed? For what do you need to repent? What will you do differently going forward? What commitment to your spiritual growth are you going to make? Is there something that you need from God in order to live His word daily? If not for yourself, for whom do you need to pray as it relates to this WOTD? What can you thank God for and/or declare in confidence according to God's word? What can you boldly and confidently ask God for according to His word? Use the space below to record your personal revelation from God about how these verses apply to you and/or write a personal prayer to God.

day 25

Romans 4:4-5: **"When people work, their wages are not a gift, but something they have earned. But people are counted righteous, not because of their work, but because of their faith in God who forgives sinners."** Employees are hired by a company to perform specific duties in exchange for compensation. Employees have a right to demand their wages because they performed their work - because they earned the right to get paid. Equally as rightful is employers' right to withhold those wages when their employees don't work; employers don't pay wages as a gift and will justly terminate an employee for not following the company's rules, sometimes in an instant. God operates differently than employers. First, God doesn't owe us anything, not even salvation. The wages that we have rightfully earned for our sinful work is death (Romans 6:23). Second, God freely gifts to us salvation (forgiveness of our sins) when we have faith in Him through Jesus Christ. It is our faith, not our works, that makes us righteous. I don't know about you, but I am so grateful to God for not paying me what I earned for my sinful work; but instead, forgiving my sins and counting me as righteous because I have faith in Him through Jesus Christ.

Personal Reflection/Application/Prayer: How has God spoken to you through today's WOTD as it relates to your life? How does today's WOTD speak to you/your situation? What was affirmed? For what do you need to repent? What will you do differently going forward? What commitment to your spiritual growth are you going to make? Is there something that you need from God in order to live His word daily? If not for yourself, for whom do you need to pray as it relates to this WOTD? What can you thank God for and/or declare in confidence according to God's word? What can you boldly and confidently ask God for according to His word? Use the space below to record your personal revelation from God about how these verses apply to you and/or write a personal prayer to God.

day 26

Romans 4:11-12: **"Circumcision was a sign that Abraham already had faith and that God had already accepted him and declared him to be righteous—even before he was circumcised. So Abraham is the spiritual father of those who have faith but have not been circumcised. They are counted as righteous because of their faith. And Abraham is also the spiritual father of those who have been circumcised, but only if they have the same kind of faith Abraham had before he was circumcised."** Too often people go through meaningless, routine acts/rituals of religion. I say "meaningless" because they're going through the motions without a faith connection to God. God instituted circumcision as an outward sign of what had already taken place in Abraham's heart (i.e., faith in God) before he went through the physical act of being circumcised. Thus, the act of circumcision by itself was meaningless without faith. It was just the cutting away of foreskin. Faith had to come first. In the same way, Jesus Christ instituted baptism as an outward sign of what has already taken place in a person's heart (i.e., faith in God through Christ) before going through the physical act of being baptized. Thus, the act of baptism itself is meaningless without faith. The only thing a person does who goes through the ritual of baptism without truly believing in Jesus Christ is get wet. Faith must come first. Just as God promised, Abraham is the spiritual father of those who have faith in God. He is the father of many nations and his descendants are as numerous as the stars in the sky and sand on the seashore. Are you in this number or did you just go through the outward act without believing by faith?

Personal Reflection/Application/Prayer: How has God spoken to you through today's WOTD as it relates to your life? How does today's WOTD speak to you/your situation? What was affirmed? For what do you need to repent? What will you do differently going forward? What commitment to your spiritual growth are you going to make? Is there something that you need from God in order to live His word daily? If not for yourself, for whom do you need to pray as it relates to this WOTD? What can you thank God for and/or declare in

confidence according to God's word? What can you boldly and confidently ask God for according to His word? Use the space below to record your personal revelation from God about how these verses apply to you and/or write a personal prayer to God.

day 27

Romans 4:16: **"So the promise is received by faith. It is given as a free gift. And we are all certain to receive it, whether or not we live according to the law of Moses, if we have faith like Abraham's. For Abraham is the father of all who believe."** The covenant relationship between God and the Jews included the Law of Moses and they were bound to live by it. The good news is that the Good News isn't just for the Jews; it is also for the Gentiles (non-Jews), those who didn't have the law of Moses as a mandate. The promise of salvation - eternal life with God - is a free gift for EVERYONE who receives it by faith in by believing in Jesus Christ. There is no set of rules that must be followed to earn salvation. In the same way that you open your hands to receive gifts from people, open your heart and receive the Lord Jesus Christ as your Lord and personal Savior by faith. Confess the Lord as yours and you will be saved. That's GOOD NEWS!!!

Personal Reflection/Application/Prayer: How has God spoken to you through today's WOTD as it relates to your life? How does today's WOTD speak to you/ your situation? What was affirmed? For what do you need to repent? What will you do differently going forward? What commitment to your spiritual growth are you going to make? Is there something that you need from God in order to live His word daily? If not for yourself, for whom do you need to pray as it relates to this WOTD? What can you thank God for and/or declare in confidence according to God's word? What can you boldly and confidently ask God for according to His word? Use the space below to record your personal revelation from God about how these verses apply to you and/or write a personal prayer to God.

day 28

Romans 4:20-22: **"Abraham never wavered in believing God's promise. In fact, his faith grew stronger, and in this he brought glory to God. He was fully convinced that God is able to do whatever he promises. And because of Abraham's faith, God counted him as righteous."** Abraham never doubted God's promise to him. In fact, his faith in God grew to the point where he believed that God was able to do whatever God said that He would do. Because of this, the bible tells us that God counted Abraham as righteous. In order for Abraham's faith to grow, he had to be in relationship with God; he had to have experience with God. Abraham left his people with no clear destination ahead - only God's word that God would show him where to go. He made some poor choices along the way, but he never doubted God's promise. He didn't project his mess-ups onto God. What about you? To what extent has your faith in God grown? What have been your experiences with God? Do you believe that God can do whatever He promises to do?

Personal Reflection/Application/Prayer: How has God spoken to you through today's WOTD as it relates to your life? How does today's WOTD speak to you/ your situation? What was affirmed? For what do you need to repent? What will you do differently going forward? What commitment to your spiritual growth are you going to make? Is there something that you need from God in order to live His word daily? If not for yourself, for whom do you need to pray as it relates to this WOTD? What can you thank God for and/or declare in confidence according to God's word? What can you boldly and confidently ask God for according to His word? Use the space below to record your personal revelation from God about how these verses apply to you and/or write a personal prayer to God.

day 29

Romans 4:23-25: **"And when God counted him as righteous, it wasn't just for Abraham's benefit. It was recorded for our benefit, too, assuring us that God will also count us as righteous if we believe in him, the one who raised Jesus our Lord from the dead. He was handed over to die because of our sins, and he was raised to life to make us right with God."** Seriously consider the fact that God was thinking about you when he called Abraham. Abraham's decision to believe in God wasn't just about him; it left implications for all people who would follow his example. God recorded Abraham's story of faith that leads to righteousness before God as assurance for ALL who believe in Jesus Christ. He gave us the roadmap to Him and it is faith in Jesus Christ alone. Get on and stay on the right road.

Personal Reflection/Application/Prayer: How has God spoken to you through today's WOTD as it relates to your life? How does today's WOTD speak to you/ your situation? What was affirmed? For what do you need to repent? What will you do differently going forward? What commitment to your spiritual growth are you going to make? Is there something that you need from God in order to live His word daily? If not for yourself, for whom do you need to pray as it relates to this WOTD? What can you thank God for and/or declare in confidence according to God's word? What can you boldly and confidently ask God for according to His word? Use the space below to record your personal revelation from God about how these verses apply to you and/or write a personal prayer to God.

day 30

Today's WOTD comes from Romans 5:1-2: **"Therefore, since we have been made right in God's sight by faith, we have peace with God because of what Jesus Christ our Lord has done for us. Because of our faith, Christ has brought us into the place of undeserved privilege where we now stand, and we confidently and joyfully look forward to sharing God's glory."** "Peace" in this passage refers to harmony between individuals.[12] Hostility stands between sinful man and God, as sin blocks our access to God the Father; in fact, God's wrath/death is our just due. Jesus gave up his life to bring peace between Father and us and restore our relationship with Him. Because of our faith in what Jesus did for us, we have direct access to Father as His children. Living in this place of "undeserved privilege" gives us confidence and joy that we will share in Father's glory. There is nothing deserving, nothing good in us in our own right that entitles us to this place of access. It is truly an undeserved privilege, one that we should never take for granted. This place of undeserved privilege should motivate us to willingly turn from anything that threatens to block/hinder our relationship with our Father in heaven. Thank Father for the peace that you have with Him through Christ; thank Father for the place of undeserved privilege that you have because of your faith in Christ. Live a Worshipful Wednesday in the Lord!

Personal Reflection/Application/Prayer: How has God spoken to you through today's WOTD as it relates to your life? How does today's WOTD speak to you/your situation? What was affirmed? For what do you need to repent? What will you do differently going forward? What commitment to your spiritual growth are you going to make? Is there something that you need from God in order to live His word daily? If not for yourself, for whom do you need to pray as it relates to this WOTD? What can you thank God for and/or declare in confidence according to God's word? What can you boldly and confidently ask God for according to His word? Use the space below to record your personal revelation from God about how these verses apply to you and/or write a personal prayer to God.

[12] https://www.blueletterbible.org/lang/lexicon/lexicon.cfm?Strongs=G1515&t=NLT

day 31

Today's WOTD comes from Romans 5:3: **"We can rejoice, too, when we run into problems and trials, for we know that they help us develop endurance."** The first part of this verse is problematic to our natural mind, so much so that we often don't get to the second part of it. Depending upon where you are in your relationship with our Father, you may be asking, "*How in the world am I supposed to rejoice when I am going through 'problems and trials'?*" I pondered the difference/connection between the two and the word "tribulations" used in most translations of this verse. *Problems and trials* describe the two aspects of tribulations.[13] *Problems* refer to the external things that challenge, press, and cause us difficulty. *Trials* refer to the internal pressure, distress, anguish, etc... that we face, often as a result of our problems, but also as a result of our internal issues. Not only do we have to contend with external factors, but we also wrestle with how they impact us internally. They can be so hard that we ask what good can possibly come from them. "*How in the world can I rejoice when I am trying to keep my head above water, when I'm trying not to curse somebody out, when I am trying to resist taking matters into my own hands or giving up altogether?*" In other words, problems and trials press our faith; but, take heart Beloved. There is a reason to rejoice IN SPITE OF (NOT because of) your problems and trials; so, don't get stuck at the first part of the verse. Press your way to the end of it. Your problems and trials serve a Kingdom purpose, which is to develop your endurance. *Endurance* refers to your staying power, your ability to persevere and stay intentionally focused on your purpose/goal despite the problems and trials you face. You might be in the midst of a problem and trial (or several of them) at this very moment. What you are going through is actually working for you even though it looks otherwise.[14] You will be stronger by the time you get on the other side IF you maintain a Kingdom perspective. Receive this spiritual truth today.

---

[13] https://www.blueletterbible.org/lang/lexicon/lexicon.cfm?Strongs=G2347&t=NLTns

[14] Romans 8:28

Choose right now to resist the temptation to wallow in misery and pity; refuse to respond in anger and blaming; refuse to nurse the devil's lies of defeat. Instead, choose to rejoice and give thanks. Thank Father for giving you a proper perspective - a Kingdom perspective - about your problems and trials.

Personal Reflection/Application/Prayer: How has God spoken to you through today's WOTD as it relates to your life? How does today's WOTD speak to you/ your situation? What was affirmed? For what do you need to repent? What will you do differently going forward? What commitment to your spiritual growth are you going to make? Is there something that you need from God in order to live His word daily? If not for yourself, for whom do you need to pray as it relates to this WOTD? What can you thank God for and/or declare in confidence according to God's word? What can you boldly and confidently ask God for according to His word? Use the space below to record your personal revelation from God about how these verses apply to you and/or write a personal prayer to God.

day 32

Romans 5:6-8: **"When we were utterly helpless, Christ came at just the right time and died for us sinners. Now, most people would not be willing to die for an upright person, though someone might perhaps be willing to die for a person who is especially good. But God showed his great love for us by sending Christ to die for us while we were still sinners."** I can tell you right now that I would not willingly give my life for people who would reject me and continue doing the very thing that I gave my life to free them from; nor would I give either of my children to die for people who would reject me, who would continue sinning after I gave the best that I had just to save them. It would be a slap in the face to me. I know that I am not the only one who feels this way, which is why the depth of God's love for us is so mind-blowing to me. God loves us in spite of, not because of, us. There were no pre-requisites for us to fulfill to get God's love.[15] Knowing that there was absolutely nothing that we could/can do to save ourselves from the penalty of sin, God sent His only Son to die for us WHILE WE WERE STILL SINNERS. Christ came and died for us even though He knew that not everyone would accept Him; yet, He did it anyway. Christ died knowing that you and I would fall short of the glory of God[16]; yet, He did it anyway. That is LOVE in its purest form - UNCONDITIONAL!

Personal Reflection/Application/Prayer: How has God spoken to you through today's WOTD as it relates to your life? How does today's WOTD speak to you/ your situation? What was affirmed? For what do you need to repent? What will you do differently going forward? What commitment to your spiritual growth are you going to make? Is there something that you need from God in order to live His word daily? If not for yourself, for whom do you need to pray as it relates to this WOTD? What can you thank God for and/or declare in confidence according to God's word? What can you boldly and confidently ask God for according to His word? Use the space below to record your personal revelation from God about how these verses apply to you and/or write a personal prayer to God.

---

[15] Ephesians 1:4-5

[16] Romans 3:23

day 33

Romans 5:9-11: **"And since we have been made right in God's sight by the blood of Christ, he will certainly save us from God's condemnation. For since our friendship with God was restored by the death of his Son while we were still his enemies, we will certainly be saved through the life of his Son. So now we can rejoice in our wonderful new relationship with God because our Lord Jesus Christ has made us friends of God."** Here is another reason to rejoice: Because of your belief in Christ's death on the cross for your sins and your acceptance of Christ as your Lord and Savior, He has made you a friend of God! You are no longer an enemy of God because of your sins; you are a friend of God because of the blood of Christ that covers your sins. GOD CALLS YOU "FRIEND"!!!! Rejoice over the best friendship you can ever have in your life.

Personal Reflection/Application/Prayer: How has God spoken to you through today's WOTD as it relates to your life? How does today's WOTD speak to you/ your situation? What was affirmed? For what do you need to repent? What will you do differently going forward? What commitment to your spiritual growth are you going to make? Is there something that you need from God in order to live His word daily? If not for yourself, for whom do you need to pray as it relates to this WOTD? What can you thank God for and/or declare in confidence according to God's word? What can you boldly and confidently ask God for according to His word? Use the space below to record your personal revelation from God about how these verses apply to you and/or write a personal prayer to God.

day 34

Romans 5:12, 14b-16: **"When Adam sinned, sin entered the world. Adam's sin brought death, so death spread to everyone, for everyone sinned... Now Adam is a symbol, a representation of Christ, who was yet to come. But there is a great difference between Adam's sin and God's gracious gift. For the sin of this one man, Adam, brought death to many. But even greater is God's wonderful grace and his gift of forgiveness to many through this other man, Jesus Christ. And the result of God's gracious gift is very different from the result of that one man's sins. For Adam's sin led to condemnation, but God's free gift leads to our being made right with God, even though we are guilty of many sins."** Just as sin entered the world through Adam's disobedience to God, salvation entered the world through Christ's obedience to God. Humanity fell through Adam; yet, is offered forgiveness through Christ. Condemnation came through Adam; reconciliation comes through Christ EVEN THOUGH WE ARE GUILTY OF MANY SINS. God's grace is amazing!

Personal Reflection/Application/Prayer: How has God spoken to you through today's WOTD as it relates to your life? How does today's WOTD speak to you/ your situation? What was affirmed? For what do you need to repent? What will you do differently going forward? What commitment to your spiritual growth are you going to make? Is there something that you need from God in order to live His word daily? If not for yourself, for whom do you need to pray as it relates to this WOTD? What can you thank God for and/or declare in confidence according to God's word? What can you boldly and confidently ask God for according to His word? Use the space below to record your personal revelation from God about how these verses apply to you and/or write a personal prayer to God.

day 35

Romans 7:17-19: **"For the sin of this one man, Adam, caused death to rule over many. But even greater is God's wonderful grace and his gift of righteousness, for all who receive it will live in triumph over sin and death through this one man, Jesus Christ. Yes, Adam's one sin brings condemnation for everyone, but Christ's one act of righteousness brings a right relationship with God and new life for everyone. Because one person disobeyed God, many became sinners. But because one other person obeyed God, many will be made righteous."** If you conscientiously think about the impact of Adam's sin and what it means for humanity - you, in particular (because you know your own sins), you will have a greater appreciation of God's grace and His gift of righteousness, as well as an understanding of our need for them, and you will thank Him constantly for them. Notice, though, that verse 19 says, "many will be made righteous." Even though ALL of us are dependent upon God's grace, accepting God's gift of righteousness is a personal choice and not everyone will accept this precious gift that gives us a "new life" in Christ. You can't make anyone accept God's gift even though you know that everyone needs it. That isn't your responsibility; your responsibility is to tell everyone you know about God's grace and His gift of righteousness through believing in and accepting Jesus Christ AND to live a life that shows YOUR gratitude for God's grace and gift.

Personal Reflection/Application/Prayer: How has God spoken to you through today's WOTD as it relates to your life? How does today's WOTD speak to you/your situation? What was affirmed? For what do you need to repent? What will you do differently going forward? What commitment to your spiritual growth are you going to make? Is there something that you need from God in order to live His word daily? If not for yourself, for whom do you need to pray as it relates to this WOTD? What can you thank God for and/or declare in confidence according to God's word? What can you boldly and confidently ask God for according to His word? Use the space below to record your personal revelation from God about how these verses apply to you and/or write a personal prayer to God.

day 36

Romans 5:20-21: **"God's law was given so that all people could see how sinful they were. But as people sinned more and more, God's wonderful grace became more abundant. So just as sin ruled over all people and brought them to death, now God's wonderful grace rules instead, giving us right standing with God and resulting in eternal life through Jesus Christ our Lord."** Before Jesus, sin ruled in the world with death and eternal torment waiting to swallow us whole. Jesus came, lived, and died to give us an option: bondage or freedom, death or life. Through Jesus Christ our Lord, EVERYONE has a choice only because of God's grace in giving us this option while we were in still our sin. What choice will you make? If you've accepted God's gift, have you opened it, read the instruction manual so that you will know how to use it in this life, and are you living by those instructions to stay free from the bondage of sin? ...OR Did you accept the gift and push it to the side without seeing how it can help you in this life because what you're experiencing in bondage to sin makes you "feel" free? If you're a Christian, there ought to be fruit hanging from your tree for the world to see as evidence that you not only accepted God's gracious gift of being made right with Him through Christ, but also that you are living the gift.

Personal Reflection/Application/Prayer: How has God spoken to you through today's WOTD as it relates to your life? How does today's WOTD speak to you/your situation? What was affirmed? For what do you need to repent? What will you do differently going forward? What commitment to your spiritual growth are you going to make? Is there something that you need from God in order to live His word daily? If not for yourself, for whom do you need to pray as it relates to this WOTD? What can you thank God for and/or declare in confidence according to God's word? What can you boldly and confidently ask God for according to His word? Use the space below to record your personal revelation from God about how these verses apply to you and/or write a personal prayer to God.

day 37

Romans 6:1-4: **"Well then, should we keep on sinning so that God can show us more and more of his wonderful grace? Of course not! Since we have died to sin, how can we continue to live in it? Or have you forgotten that when we were joined with Christ Jesus in baptism, we joined him in his death? For we died and were buried with Christ by baptism. And just as Christ was raised from the dead by the glorious power of the Father, now we also may live new lives."** As recipients of God's grace and gift of eternal life through Christ Jesus, Christians have a CHOICE whether to continue intentionally living in sin or not. As long as the world as we know it exists, sin will exist. However, the power of sin in a person's life ends when he/she accepts Jesus Christ as Lord and Savior.[17] Through God's gift of grace, a person gets a new life in Christ. Baptism symbolizes the death of the old sin-filled and sin-controlled person who goes into the water and the raising up of a new life in Christ who comes up out of the water. Not that temptation won't come, not that it will always be easy to say no to sin all the time (especially, as a new believer), and not that you won't ever sin again (because we all fall short from time-to-time[18]), BUT Christians should ALWAYS remember that God's grace on your life FREES you from the power of sin to control you. God's grace gives you CHOICE. God's grace should NEVER BE TAKEN FOR GRANTED and used as an excuse to do what you know displeases God.

Personal Reflection/Application/Prayer: How has God spoken to you through today's WOTD as it relates to your life? How does today's WOTD speak to you/ your situation? What was affirmed? For what do you need to repent? What will you do differently going forward? What commitment to your spiritual growth are you going to make? Is there something that you need from God in order to live His word daily? If not for yourself, for whom do you need to pray as it relates to this

---

[17] Romans 6:6-7

[18] Romans 3:23

WOTD? What can you thank God for and/or declare in confidence according to God's word? What can you boldly and confidently ask God for according to His word? Use the space below to record your personal revelation from God about how these verses apply to you and/or write a personal prayer to God.

day 38

Romans 6:6-7: **"We know that our old sinful selves were crucified with Christ so that sin might lose its power in our lives. We are no longer slaves to sin. For when we died with Christ we were set free from the power of sin."** Sadly, many Christians remain in a posture of slavery to sin even though Christ unlocked the chains that held them bound. Christ took the power of sin from over your life; however, IT IS UP TO YOU to change your posture. Whom the Son has set free is free indeed[19]; so, refuse to be a slave to sin. Instead, declare out loud: "I'm free. Praise the Lord, I'm free. I'm no longer a slave to sin!" Now, live in that reality to the glory of God!

Personal Reflection/Application/Prayer: How has God spoken to you through today's WOTD as it relates to your life? How does today's WOTD speak to you/ your situation? What was affirmed? For what do you need to repent? What will you do differently going forward? What commitment to your spiritual growth are you going to make? Is there something that you need from God in order to live His word daily? If not for yourself, for whom do you need to pray as it relates to this WOTD? What can you thank God for and/or declare in confidence according to God's word? What can you boldly and confidently ask God for according to His word? Use the space below to record your personal revelation from God about how these verses apply to you and/or write a personal prayer to God.

[19] John 8:34-36

day 39

Romans 6:8-11: **"And since we died with Christ, we know we will also live with him. We are sure of this because Christ was raised from the dead, and he will never die again. Death no longer has any power over him. When he died, he died once to break the power of sin. But now that he lives, he lives for the glory of God. So you also should consider yourselves to be dead to the power of sin and alive to God through Christ Jesus."** Jesus Christ, not this world, sets the standard for Christians. When Christ died on the cross for the sins of humanity, He broke the power of sin over the lives of those who would accept Him then, now, and in the future.[20] Your old sin-filled, sin-controlled self died with Him. When God raised Christ from the dead, everyone who would accept Him then, now, and in the future begins a new life - a life dead to the power of sin and alive to God. If you are saved, rejoice over the fact that you are dead to the power of sin; you have to accept what the devil dishes out to you. You are alive to God! If you are not saved, there is no time like the present to accept God's love for you through Jesus Christ and begin a new spiritual life of freedom! It is the most important decision you will make and it will transform your physical, emotional, and mental life!

Personal Reflection/Application/Prayer: How has God spoken to you through today's WOTD as it relates to your life? How does today's WOTD speak to you/ your situation? What was affirmed? For what do you need to repent? What will you do differently going forward? What commitment to your spiritual growth are you going to make? Is there something that you need from God in order to live His word daily? If not for yourself, for whom do you need to pray as it relates to this WOTD? What can you thank God for and/or declare in confidence according to God's word? What can you boldly and confidently ask God for according to His word? Use the space below to record your personal revelation from God about how these verses apply to you and/or write a personal prayer to God.

[20] Romans 6:6-7

day 40

Romans 6:12-14: **"Do not let sin control the way you live; do not give in to sinful desires. Do not let any part of your body become an instrument of evil to serve sin. Instead, give yourselves completely to God, for you were dead, but now you have new life. So use your whole body as an instrument to do what is right for the glory of God. Sin is no longer your master, for you no longer live under the requirements of the law. Instead, you live under the freedom of God's grace."** "Do not let…", "give", and "use" indicate that you have a choice in how you live your life now that Christ has broken the power of sin over your life. Sin will use any part of your body that you allow to be influenced by the devil: your eyes, mouth, ears, heart, hands, feet, etc., Your body is the temple of the Holy Spirit.[21] Every part of your body is sacred and is to be set apart for use by God and God alone[22]; so, be intentional about what you do with and to it AND what you allow others to do with and to it. Receive this truth in your spirit and let your daily VERBAL declaration be: *"Because of God's grace, sin is no longer my master. I am living a new life and I choose today to not let sin control the way I live. The Holy Spirit lives in me and I choose this day not to let any part of my body become an instrument of evil to serve sin. I live under the freedom of God's grace and I choose this day to use my whole body as an instrument to do what is right for the glory of God."* Write this declaration on several index cards and keep it with you. Pull it out whenever you are tempted to give in to sin and declare this word of God aloud over your life. Keeping this truth about you before you will remind you of who you are and that you have a purpose.

Personal Reflection/Application/Prayer: How has God spoken to you through today's WOTD as it relates to your life? How does today's WOTD speak to you/ your situation? What was affirmed? For what do you need to repent? What will you do differently going forward? What commitment to your spiritual growth are you going to make? Is there something that you need from God in order to live His word daily? If not for yourself, for whom do you need to pray as it relates to this

---

[21] 1 Corinthians 6:19

[22] 1 Corinthians 6:20

WOTD? What can you thank God for and/or declare in confidence according to God's word? What can you boldly and confidently ask God for according to His word? Use the space below to record your personal revelation from God about how these verses apply to you and/or write a personal prayer to God.

day 41

Romans 6:15-16: "**Well then, since God's grace has set us free from the law, does that mean we can go on sinning? Of course not! Don't you realize that you become the slave of whatever you choose to obey? You can be a slave to sin, which leads to death, or you can obey God, which leads to righteous living.**" Unbelievers are slaves to sin - no ifs, ands, or buts about it. They don't have a choice. Believers do. If you, as a Christian, are CHOOSING TO LIVE any area of your life outside of the will of God, YOU HAVE CHOSEN TO BECOME A SLAVE TO SIN whether you want to admit it or not. In fact, denying, minimizing, and/or dismissing what you know is your sinful behavior is a tell-tell sign that you are bound to sin. The word of God is clear: We become slaves of whatever we choose to obey. We have two choices: slavery (obedience) to sin = death OR slavery (obedience) to God = righteous living. Whose slave have you chosen to become?

Personal Reflection/Application/Prayer: How has God spoken to you through today's WOTD as it relates to your life? How does today's WOTD speak to you/ your situation? What was affirmed? For what do you need to repent? What will you do differently going forward? What commitment to your spiritual growth are you going to make? Is there something that you need from God in order to live His word daily? If not for yourself, for whom do you need to pray as it relates to this WOTD? What can you thank God for and/or declare in confidence according to God's word? What can you boldly and confidently ask God for according to His word? Use the space below to record your personal revelation from God about how these verses apply to you and/or write a personal prayer to God.

day 42

Romans 6:19: **"Because of the weakness of your human nature, I am using the illustration of slavery to help you understand all this. Previously, you let yourselves be slaves to impurity and lawlessness, which led ever deeper into sin. Now you must give yourselves to be slaves to righteous living so that you will become holy."** There is a difference between sinning and living in sin. A sin is ANYTHING that displeases God - that goes against the principles He has established for us to live by. God, and God alone, sets the order for what is right and what is wrong - for what is sin and what isn't - even if you don't like it. Living in sin refers to that place of perpetual and even intentional rebellion against God in how we live. The danger of unchecked and unrepented for sin is that it leads you into deeper sin until you are so far away from God that you don't know how to get back to Him. The good news is that it isn't too late for you to choose to live righteously. Through God's word, you know that every Christian has a choice when it comes to living in sin because Jesus broke the power of sin over our lives.[23] This means that every second that you breathe is your "Now" moment to choose to repent of (turn away from) sin and sinful living. Every second that you breathe is your "Now" moment to choose to turn back to Christ and live in the authority that you have in Him. Every second that you breathe is your "Now" moment to choose to be slaves to righteous living so that you will become holy. The next second, minute, hour, day, week, month, or year isn't promised to you. What will you choose in your "Now" moment?

Personal Reflection/Application/Prayer: How has God spoken to you through today's WOTD as it relates to your life? How does today's WOTD speak to you/ your situation? What was affirmed? For what do you need to repent? What will you do differently going forward? What commitment to your spiritual growth are you going to make? Is there something that you need from God in order to live His word daily? If not for yourself, for whom do you need to pray as it relates to this

[23] Romans 6:6-7

WOTD? What can you thank God for and/or declare in confidence according to God's word? What can you boldly and confidently ask God for according to His word? Use the space below to record your personal revelation from God about how these verses apply to you and/or write a personal prayer to God.

day 43

Romans 6:23: **"For the wages of sin is death, but the gift of God is eternal life through Christ Jesus our Lord."** The word of God is explicitly clear about how sin separates us from God, about the penalty for sin, and about God's provision to restore humanity to a right relationship with Him through Jesus Christ. I don't know about you; but, when I think about the fact that I deserve death for my sins; yet, God loves me so much that He gives me eternal life through Jesus Christ, I can't help but thank Him for His love, grace, and mercy towards me. When I think about the fact that I deserve death for my sins; yet, God gives me eternal life, the more determined I am to give Him the glory through how I live my life. How do you feel knowing that YOU DESERVE DEATH for your sins; YET, GOD GIVES you ETERNAL LIFE through Christ Jesus our Lord? How do you show God that you appreciate the gift of eternal life that He has provided for you through Christ Jesus our Lord?

Personal Reflection/Application/Prayer: How has God spoken to you through today's WOTD as it relates to your life? How does today's WOTD speak to you/ your situation? What was affirmed? For what do you need to repent? What will you do differently going forward? What commitment to your spiritual growth are you going to make? Is there something that you need from God in order to live His word daily? If not for yourself, for whom do you need to pray as it relates to this WOTD? What can you thank God for and/or declare in confidence according to God's word? What can you boldly and confidently ask God for according to His word? Use the space below to record your personal revelation from God about how these verses apply to you and/or write a personal prayer to God.

day 44

Romans 7:4: **"So, my dear brothers and sisters, this is the point: You died to the power of the law when you died with Christ. And now you are united with the one who was raised from the dead. As a result, we can produce a harvest of good deeds for God."** Doing good deeds will not earn you salvation; salvation is a gift given to you by God when you put your faith in Christ. Because you are in a relationship with Jesus Christ, you can do good deeds for God. As you prepare to begin your day, ask the Holy Spirit to show you how you can produce good deeds for the Father today. Ask how you can be a blessing to the Kingdom of God; then, follow the Holy Spirit's leading and thank God for choosing to use you for His glory.

Personal Reflection/Application/Prayer: How has God spoken to you through today's WOTD as it relates to your life? How does today's WOTD speak to you/your situation? What was affirmed? For what do you need to repent? What will you do differently going forward? What commitment to your spiritual growth are you going to make? Is there something that you need from God in order to live His word daily? If not for yourself, for whom do you need to pray as it relates to this WOTD? What can you thank God for and/or declare in confidence according to God's word? What can you boldly and confidently ask God for according to His word? Use the space below to record your personal revelation from God about how these verses apply to you and/or write a personal prayer to God.

day 45

Romans 7:5-6: **"When we were controlled by our old sinful nature, sinful desires were at work within us, and the law aroused these evil desires that produced a harvest of sinful deeds, resulting in death. But now we have been released from the law, for we died to it and are no longer captive to its power. Now we can serve God, not in the old way of obeying the letter of the law, but in the new way of living in the Spirit."** The law points out your sinful nature. The temptation that comes from trying to live the letter of the law is wanting what the law says is wrong because that is what the law draws your attention to. That's pressure! Focusing on the letter of the law is rule-based religion; living your life led by the Spirit of God is *relationship*. As you read, study, and meditate on God's word and how it applies to your life, it becomes a part of you and the Holy Spirit will bring it to your remembrance; especially, as you contemplate your decisions. Thank God that you don't have to be preoccupied with the rules of religion. Because you are in Christ, you have Holy Spirit to lead you in living for God.

Personal Reflection/Application/Prayer: How has God spoken to you through today's WOTD as it relates to your life? How does today's WOTD speak to you/ your situation? What was affirmed? For what do you need to repent? What will you do differently going forward? What commitment to your spiritual growth are you going to make? Is there something that you need from God in order to live His word daily? If not for yourself, for whom do you need to pray as it relates to this WOTD? What can you thank God for and/or declare in confidence according to God's word? What can you boldly and confidently ask God for according to His word? Use the space below to record your personal revelation from God about how these verses apply to you and/or write a personal prayer to God.

day 46

Romans 7:12-13: **"But still, the law itself is holy, and its commands are holy and right and good. But how can that be? Did the law, which is good, cause my death? Of course not! Sin used what was good to bring about my condemnation to death. So we can see how terrible sin really is. It uses God's good commands for its own evil purposes."** These verses show the simplest contrast between God's law and sin. God's law is perfect, good, and right. There is nothing wrong or harmful about following God's law. Sin, on the other hand, is terrible and perverse. Sin's motive is purely evil. Sin has as its ultimate goal for you and me to be condemned to death. PERIOD. Sin takes the good law that God gave us to live by and twists it in our minds (usually by making us feel restricted or as if we're missing out on something good) to get us to do wrong instead of right, evil instead of good because it knows that the payment for sin is death. It leads to condemnation and eternal damnation. Thank God for loving humanity so much that He gave His only begotten Son to die in our place, that whoever believes in His Son, Jesus Christ, would not be condemned to eternal damnation but would have eternal life.[24] Thank God for sending Jesus to save humanity. Thank God that there is no condemnation for those who are in Christ Jesus.[25] Thank God for His unconditional love, amazing grace, and enduring mercy in our lives.[26]

Personal Reflection/Application/Prayer: How has God spoken to you through today's WOTD as it relates to your life? How does today's WOTD speak to you/ your situation? What was affirmed? For what do you need to repent? What will you do differently going forward? What commitment to your spiritual growth are you going to make? Is there something that you need from God in order to live His word daily? If not for yourself, for whom do you need to pray as it relates to this

[24] John 3:16-17

[25] Romans 8:1

[26] Psalm 136; 1 Chronicles 16:34

WOTD? What can you thank God for and/or declare in confidence according to God's word? What can you boldly and confidently ask God for according to His word? Use the space below to record your personal revelation from God about how these verses apply to you and/or write a personal prayer to God.

day 47

Romans 7:14-17: **"So the trouble is not with the law, for it is spiritual and good. The trouble is with me, for I am all too human, a slave to sin. I don't really understand myself, for I want to do what is right, but I don't do it. Instead, I do what I hate. But if I know that what I am doing is wrong, this shows that I agree that the law is good. So I am not the one doing wrong; it is sin living in me that does it."** I'M GUILTY! I can't tell you how many times in my life that I've asked myself, "What am I doing? Why in the world did I do that?" If you are honest with yourself, you must also raise your hand to say that these verses [and the ones for the rest of the week] describe your past and/or present inner struggle. Even though you knew that it was wrong the first time you did it and even though you felt guilty about doing it, you found/find yourself drawn back to it again - almost against your will - as if you can't help yourself. The struggle between your faith and your flesh - between doing what you know is right and wrong - is real. That's how powerful sin is. That's why you can't play around with the temptation to sin. If this is where you find yourself currently, admit it to yourself; confess it to God; ask God to deliver you from this bondage to sin, and give you the strength to resist the devil. Before doing or saying anything in the face of temptation, pause and pray. If you do so sincerely, trust that God will answer because He will. I know that He will because He did it for me!

Personal Reflection/Application/Prayer: How has God spoken to you through today's WOTD as it relates to your life? How does today's WOTD speak to you/your situation? What was affirmed? For what do you need to repent? What will you do differently going forward? What commitment to your spiritual growth are you going to make? Is there something that you need from God in order to live His word daily? If not for yourself, for whom do you need to pray as it relates to this WOTD? What can you thank God for and/or declare in confidence according to God's word? What can you boldly and confidently ask God for according to His word? Use the space below to record your personal revelation from God about how these verses apply to you and/or write a personal prayer to God.

day 48

Romans 7:18-20: **"And I know that nothing good lives in me, that is, in my sinful nature. I want to do what is right, but I can't. I want to do what is good, but I don't. I don't want to do what is wrong, but I do it anyway. But if I do what I don't want to do, I am not really the one doing wrong; it is sin living in me that does it."** Satan doesn't walk away from you just because you accepted Jesus as Lord and Savior. While your salvation is secure, his assignment is still to steal, kill, and destroy in your life. He is determined to keep you in spiritual bondage to him even though Jesus took his power. Where does his plan start? It starts in your mind where he plants seeds of lies. Without realizing it, you fertilize those lie seeds every time you think about them. The more your thoughts settle on them, the more subtly drawn into them you become. You know what you need to do, but you listen to that voice (whether yours or someone else's) saying "just this once", "I'll try it", "one more time", "Everyone else is doing it", "No one will know", "Why should I have to…?", etc. Sin is real and nothing to be played with. The inner struggle is real! I'M GUILTY! One thing is clear: Not one of us is a match for the devil on our own. You were meant to win, but you'll never win under the power of sin. You need a power greater than you and the enemy. Take your struggle with your sinful nature to God in prayer. Ask God to deliver you from this bondage to sin, to give you the strength to resist the devil. Before doing or saying anything in the face of temptation, pause and pray. If you do so sincerely, trust that God will answer because He will. I know that He will because He did it for me!

Personal Reflection/Application/Prayer: How has God spoken to you through today's WOTD as it relates to your life? How does today's WOTD speak to you/ your situation? What was affirmed? For what do you need to repent? What will you do differently going forward? What commitment to your spiritual growth are you going to make? Is there something that you need from God in order to live His word daily? If not for yourself, for whom do you need to pray as it relates to this

WOTD? What can you thank God for and/or declare in confidence according to God's word? What can you boldly and confidently ask God for according to His word? Use the space below to record your personal revelation from God about how these verses apply to you and/or write a personal prayer to God.

day 49

Romans 7:21-25: **"I have discovered this principle of life—that when I want to do what is right, I inevitably do what is wrong. I love God's law with all my heart. But there is another power within me that is at war with my mind. This power makes me a slave to the sin that is still within me. Oh, what a miserable person I am! Who will free me from this life that is dominated by sin and death? Thank God! The answer is in Jesus Christ our Lord. So you see how it is: In my mind I really want to obey God's law, but because of my sinful nature I am a slave to sin."** This is the root of our struggle with sin: "There is another power within [us] that is at war with [our] mind." While satan is not all-powerful, he is powerful. God created him to be that way - that is - powerful for a good reason in his service to Almighty God. When God kicked Lucifer out of heaven to the earth, he changed this fallen angel's name to satan, but he didn't take his power from him. The devil uses the power that God gave him to do good to, instead, influence us to rebel against God like he did. Apart from Jesus, you and I are powerless to resist this demonic power that makes us a slave to the sin within us. Thanks to Adam, all of us are born into sin and our sinful nature makes us gravitate away from God. BUT thanks to Jesus, the power of sin is broken off of our lives when we believe in and accept Him as Lord and Savior of our lives. Our sinful nature does not go away once we become saved, but we now have the choice to die to our sinful nature every time we say no to sin. The more you lean into God's love for you, wear God's armor[27], build yourself up with His word (which is your offensive and defensive weapon to fight against the enemy), and use your weapon of prayer: thanksgiving, praise, and petition), you will be able to resist the devil. You can look your temptation to do wrong in the face and say, "I AM DEAD TO YOU!!!" Then, turn around and walk away thanking the Lord for giving you the strength and courage to resist sin. Eventually, the devil will leave you alone in that area and go look for another weakness of yours to exploit so he can come back and try again.

[27] Ephesians 6:10-17

KEEP RESISTING AND THE DEVIL WILL KEEP FLEEING.[28] Thank God for giving you an understanding of our common struggle with sin at its root. Now, give God praise for giving you the armor and weapons to stand and fight. Praise God that you are dead to sin and alive in Christ!

Personal Reflection/Application/Prayer: How has God spoken to you through today's WOTD as it relates to your life? How does today's WOTD speak to you/ your situation? What was affirmed? For what do you need to repent? What will you do differently going forward? What commitment to your spiritual growth are you going to make? Is there something that you need from God in order to live His word daily? If not for yourself, for whom do you need to pray as it relates to this WOTD? What can you thank God for and/or declare in confidence according to God's word? What can you boldly and confidently ask God for according to His word? Use the space below to record your personal revelation from God about how these verses apply to you and/or write a personal prayer to God.

[28] James 4:7

day 50

Romans 8:1-2: **"So now there is no condemnation for those who belong to Christ Jesus. And because you belong to him, the power of the life-giving Spirit has freed you from the power of sin that leads to death."** Picture this scene: You are in the Court of Heaven and your accuser, the devil, is presenting all of your sins to God.[29] Every lie you've ever told, everything that you thought you did in the dark away from watching eyes, every instance of your disobedience to God is being presented to God in full color and detail. Satan rests his case, confident that you will be found guilty and sentenced to death. Jesus Christ, the Mediator and our Advocate[30], stands up and says that the devil has presented the facts. The evidence speaks for itself. You did everything the devil said you did. However, the devil forgot to include the most important fact when presenting his case. You repented for these sins and belong to Jesus. His blood testifies on your behalf. God the Judge[31] looks back at the list of your sins and sees the blood of Jesus covering them all. He looks up and everyone in the courtroom awaits the verdict.[32] God renders a NOT GUILTY verdict on the grounds that you belong to Christ Jesus and His blood covers your sin. The Holy Spirit frees you to do God's will. ~ This happens every single day. You are rightfully accused by satan and graciously acquitted by God because of your repentance and relationship with Jesus Christ. Jesus died so that you could live. His blood covers your sins so that you are made right in God's eyes. Don't ever take the Lord's sacrifice for you for granted. Determine to live the rest of your life free to do God's will and receive God's blessings.

Personal Reflection/Application/Prayer: How has God spoken to you through today's WOTD as it relates to your life? How does today's WOTD speak to you/ your situation? What was affirmed? For what do you need to repent? What will you do differently going forward? What commitment to your spiritual growth are

[29] Revelation 12:10

[30] 1 Timothy 2:5; 1 John 2:1

[31] Hebrews 12:23; Revelation 4:3

[32] Revelation 4:4; 6:9

you going to make? Is there something that you need from God in order to live His word daily? If not for yourself, for whom do you need to pray as it relates to this WOTD? What can you thank God for and/or declare in confidence according to God's word? What can you boldly and confidently ask God for according to His word? Use the space below to record your personal revelation from God about how these verses apply to you and/or write a personal prayer to God.

day 51

Romans 8:3b-4: ***"So God did what the law could not do. He sent his own Son in a body like the bodies we sinners have. And in that body God declared an end to sin's control over us by giving his Son as a sacrifice for our sins. He did this so that the just requirement of the law would be fully satisfied for us, who no longer follow our sinful nature but instead follow the Spirit."*** The divine nature of Jesus knew no sin. So that Jesus could identify with our sinful nature as humans, God sent him in a human body.[33] Jesus knew and understood the struggles and sinfulness of our flesh because of this; yet, He did not sin.[34] There is nothing that any of us can experience in this life - no pain, no temptation, no loss, no frustration, no rejection, etc.... - that Jesus does not understand. He faced them all; yet, He did not sin. This made Him the perfect sacrifice - the perfect sin offering - to end sin's control over us and make us right with God. Because of Jesus' sacrifice, you have a choice of what/whom you will follow: your sinful nature or the Spirit. Are you following the Holy Spirit's leading in every area of your life or are there some areas in which you are following your sinful nature? Jesus didn't give His life for part of you; He gave His life for ALL of you. Surrender ALL of you to Him today and ask God to break the hold of your sinful nature off you by His Spirit.

Personal Reflection/Application/Prayer: How has God spoken to you through today's WOTD as it relates to your life? How does today's WOTD speak to you/ your situation? What was affirmed? For what do you need to repent? What will you do differently going forward? What commitment to your spiritual growth are you going to make? Is there something that you need from God in order to live His word daily? If not for yourself, for whom do you need to pray as it relates to this WOTD? What can you thank God for and/or declare in confidence according to God's word? What can you boldly and confidently ask God for according to His word? Use the space below to record your personal revelation from God about how these verses apply to you and/or write a personal prayer to God.

---

[33] John 1:14; Philippians 2:6-7

[34] 2 Corinthians 5:21

day 52

Romans 8:5-6: **"Those who are dominated by the sinful nature think about sinful things, but those who are controlled by the Holy Spirit think about things that please the Spirit. So letting your sinful nature control your mind leads to death. But letting the Spirit control your mind leads to life and peace."** Your mind is a battlefield. Before coming into a relationship with Jesus Christ, all of us are "dominated" by our sinful nature. After coming into a relationship with Christ, our sinful nature still exists; however, we have authority over it by the power of the Holy Spirit. As such, we don't have to "let" it control us. Have you ever had an ungodly thought cross your mind; especially, since you've been saved? You wonder from where in the world did it come and, at the same time, are glad that no one could read your mind. That's your sinful nature trying to gain control of your thoughts to get you to sin. The enemy is so intent on gaining yardage in your mind that he will even send ungodly thoughts in the middle of your prayers, while you're reading your Bible, while you're in church, etc.... You have to check the root of your thoughts quickly; otherwise, you risk allowing the enemy to push his way back into the living room of your mind. Entertaining those thoughts can lead you away from God; so, you have to check yourself before you wreck yourself. Quickly cast ungodly thoughts down, repent, and ask the Holy Spirit to renew your mind. Declare your freedom in the Spirit and live it in the natural. The more we surrender to and obey the Holy Spirit's leading in our lives, the less power our sinful nature has over our thoughts and actions. Living our lives led by the Holy Spirit enables us to be at peace with God.

Personal Reflection/Application/Prayer: How has God spoken to you through today's WOTD as it relates to your life? How does today's WOTD speak to you/ your situation? What was affirmed? For what do you need to repent? What will you do differently going forward? What commitment to your spiritual growth are you going to make? Is there something that you need from God in order to live His word daily? If not for yourself, for whom do you need to pray as it relates to this

WOTD? What can you thank God for and/or declare in confidence according to God's word? What can you boldly and confidently ask God for according to His word? Use the space below to record your personal revelation from God about how these verses apply to you and/or write a personal prayer to God.

day 53

Romans 8:7-9: **"For the sinful nature is always hostile to God. It never did obey God's laws, and it never will. That's why those who are still under the control of their sinful nature can never please God. But you are not controlled by your sinful nature. You are controlled by the Spirit if you have the Spirit of God living in you. (And remember that those who do not have the Spirit of Christ living in them do not belong to God at all.)"** Unbelievers do not belong to God and can never please God. This may sound shocking to you because of the unbelievers you know who are nice, good-deed-doing people. These people may even believe that there is a higher power - that God is real; however, they have never accepted Jesus Christ as their Lord and Savior. As such, they do not have the Spirit of God living in them, leading them. They are led by their sinful nature, which is ALWAYS hostile to God. God places the Holy Spirit on the inside of believers as proof that believers belong to Him. The Holy Spirit leads/guides the lives of believers; however, the Holy Spirit does not take away believers' right to choose. As a believer, thank God for giving you His Spirit as the seal on your spiritual adoption papers as proof that you have been adopted into His family. Thank God for giving you His Spirit to lead and guide you in this life where sin abounds and your sinful nature constantly looks for an opening to regain control of your life. Thank God that you can ask the Holy Spirit to help you in your weakness to resist your sinful nature, and can choose to tell your sinful nature, "No". Perhaps, you've said "Yes" to your sinful nature and the guilt and shame of it is causing you to try to avoid God. If that's you, that voice of avoidance is the enemy. God is omnipresent. He saw you when you were toying with the decision to sin, when you decided to sin, while you were sinning, and He sees you now. The Holy Spirit is right where you are, telling you to repent, turn around, and come back on the right path. God is waiting to forgive and restore you because you belong to Him. He loves you dearly, and He wants nothing but the absolute best for you. Thank your Father in Heaven for that.

Personal Reflection/Application/Prayer: How has God spoken to you through today's WOTD as it relates to your life? How does today's WOTD speak to you/

your situation? What was affirmed? For what do you need to repent? What will you do differently going forward? What commitment to your spiritual growth are you going to make? Is there something that you need from God in order to live His word daily? If not for yourself, for whom do you need to pray as it relates to this WOTD? What can you thank God for and/or declare in confidence according to God's word? What can you boldly and confidently ask God for according to His word? Use the space below to record your personal revelation from God about how these verses apply to you and/or write a personal prayer to God.

day 54

Romans 8:10-11: **"And Christ lives within you, so even though your body will die because of sin, the Spirit gives you life because you have been made right with God. The Spirit of God, who raised Jesus from the dead, lives in you. And just as God raised Christ Jesus from the dead, he will give life to your mortal bodies by this same Spirit living within you."** We are spiritual beings who live in a human body on this earth. Our time on this earth in this body has a set time span that God, alone, knows. One day, this earthly body will die. However, our spirits will continue to live. To those who have been made right with God by His Spirit, who lives in believers here on earth as proof that we belong to Him, God will give eternal life. Receive this truth about yourself if you have God's Spirit living on the inside of you: Your salvation is secure; you couldn't earn it to get it and you can't earn it to keep it. You have been given this priceless gift by His grace. You have been adopted into the family of faith; you are a son/daughter of the Most High God, a joint heir with Christ; YOU BELONG. Your eternity is secure. You don't have to wonder whether you will go to Heaven when you die. God will give you a new body in glory by His Spirit. HALLELUJAH!!!! THANK YOU, JESUS!!! If you haven't accepted Jesus Christ as your Lord and Savior, there is no better time than right now for you to admit to God that you are a sinner, repent of your sins, confess Jesus is Lord, and believe in your heart that God raised Him from the dead. By believing in your heart, you are made right with God. By confessing with your mouth, you are saved and adopted into the family of faith.[35]

Personal Reflection/Application/Prayer: How has God spoken to you through today's WOTD as it relates to your life? How does today's WOTD speak to you/ your situation? What was affirmed? For what do you need to repent? What will you do differently going forward? What commitment to your spiritual growth are you going to make? Is there something that you need from God in order to live His word daily? If not for yourself, for whom do you need to pray as it relates to this

[35] Romans 10:9-10

WOTD? What can you thank God for and/or declare in confidence according to God's word? What can you boldly and confidently ask God for according to His word? Use the space below to record your personal revelation from God about how these verses apply to you and/or write a personal prayer to God.

day 55

Romans 8:12-14: **"Therefore, dear brothers and sisters, you have no obligation to do what your sinful nature urges you to do. For if you live by its dictates, you will die. But if through the power of the Spirit you put to death the deeds of your sinful nature, you will live. For all who are led by the Spirit of God are children of God."** YOU CAN IGNORE TEMPTATION. *Obligation* in this text comes from the Greek word that means "debtor; one who owes another".[36] Listen, if you are a Christian, you owe your sinful nature ABSOLUTELY NOTHING. You don't have to do anything that it says. Your obligation is to God, who gives you life, identity, and power by His Spirit. Temptation will come your way today, tomorrow, and at various other times throughout your life. Child of God, use the power that YOU ALREADY HAVE in the Spirit to tell temptation, "I AM DEAD TO YOU!" Ignore its nagging and begging BECAUSE YOU CAN. Then, thank God for giving you the power to ignore temptation. You are led by the Spirit; so, live like it today and every day to the glory of God.

Personal Reflection/Application/Prayer: How has God spoken to you through today's WOTD as it relates to your life? How does today's WOTD speak to you/ your situation? What was affirmed? For what do you need to repent? What will you do differently going forward? What commitment to your spiritual growth are you going to make? Is there something that you need from God in order to live His word daily? If not for yourself, for whom do you need to pray as it relates to this WOTD? What can you thank God for and/or declare in confidence according to God's word? What can you boldly and confidently ask God for according to His word? Use the space below to record your personal revelation from God about how these verses apply to you and/or write a personal prayer to God.

[36] https://www.blueletterbible.org/lexicon/g3781/kjv/tr/0-1/

day 56

Romans 8:15: **"So you have not received a spirit that makes you fearful slaves. Instead, you received God's Spirit when he adopted you as his own children. Now we call him, "Abba, Father."** "Abba" means "father" in Aramaic and its context is an intimate, close relationship. For us, we would use "Daddy" or "Dad". So many people struggle with their identity, self-worth, validation, and sense of belonging because they didn't know or have a close, intimate relationship with their biological parents (whether or not they were physically present). This internal struggle is magnified if the biological father refused to even acknowledge being the father. This silent insecurity is just the fertile ground that Satan looks for to plant weeds that lead to bondage and destruction. BUT, thanks be to God that He leaves no question as to who His children are. The Holy Spirit is the birthmark of God's children, validating that we belong to Him. He leaves no question as to the close, intimate relationship that He desires to have with us. God isn't just "Father God"; He's "Daddy". We can go to Abba when we fall down and hurt ourselves. We can go to Abba when others don't treat us fairly and hurt our feelings. We can go to Abba when others reject us. We can go to Abba when we're sick. We can go to Abba when we don't know what to do. We can go to Abba when we mess up. We can go to Abba with our good news. I could go on and on. No matter the situation, we can go to Abba confident that He won't disown us, confident that He will take us in His loving arms, confident that He will fix it, confident that He will tell us what to do, and confident that He will always be here for us.

Personal Reflection/Application/Prayer: How has God spoken to you through today's WOTD as it relates to your life? How does today's WOTD speak to you/your situation? What was affirmed? For what do you need to repent? What will you do differently going forward? What commitment to your spiritual growth are you going to make? Is there something that you need from God in order to live His word daily? If not for yourself, for whom do you need to pray as it relates to this

WOTD? What can you thank God for and/or declare in confidence according to God's word? What can you boldly and confidently ask God for according to His word? Use the space below to record your personal revelation from God about how these verses apply to you and/or write a personal prayer to God.

day 57

Romans 8:16-18: **"For His Spirit joins with our spirit to affirm that we are God's children. And since we are his children, we are his heirs. In fact, together with Christ we are heirs of God's glory. But if we are to share his glory, we must also share his suffering. Yet what we suffer now is nothing compared to the glory he will reveal to us later."** God's promises are our inheritance just as they are Christ's. Every promise of protection, provision, comfort, elevation, direction, etc... EVERY PROMISE God made in His word to His children is our inheritance. This - we love to embrace and shout about, and we should. At the same time, we must understand that we also inherit suffering in this life. Jesus suffered because of who He was and what He stood for. As Christians, we, too, will endure our share of suffering in this life. We represent Jesus Christ in a world that is anti-Christ. Sin is prevalent in this world, and we are surrounded by temptations to turn away from righteous, godly living. We are attacked because we refuse to conform to the world's way of living and thinking. We are challenged not to become complacent. We are going to go through difficulties in this life. Yet, we are encouraged to stand firm in our faith because something glorious is coming after our suffering is over. It will be so glorious that our suffering will seem like nothing; it will pale in comparison to the glory that Christ will reveal to us later. So, be encouraged no matter what you go through in this life. Affirm out loud in the middle of your struggles, "What I am going through now is nothing compared to the glory Christ will reveal to me later."

Personal Reflection/Application/Prayer: How has God spoken to you through today's WOTD as it relates to your life? How does today's WOTD speak to you/your situation? What was affirmed? For what do you need to repent? What will you do differently going forward? What commitment to your spiritual growth are you going to make? Is there something that you need from God in order to live His word daily? If not for yourself, for whom do you need to pray as it relates to this WOTD? What can you thank God for and/or declare in confidence according to God's word? What can you boldly and confidently ask God for according to His word? Use the space below to record your personal revelation from God about how these verses apply to you and/or write a personal prayer to God.

day 58

Romans 8:26-27: **"And the Holy Spirit helps us in our weakness. For example, we don't know what God wants us to pray for. But the Holy Spirit prays for us with groanings that cannot be expressed in words. And the Father who knows all hearts knows what the Spirit is saying, for the Spirit pleads for us believers in harmony with God's own will."** Have you ever not known what to pray for when you go to Abba? Have you ever not prayed because you didn't feel as if you knew the right words to say to our Father in Heaven? If so, I have good news for you today. God knew that you wouldn't and made provision for it. The Holy Spirit has a prayer language and is present every time you pray, filtering and translating your words into prayers of God's will for your life. So, don't ever worry or feel less than because your prayers don't sound like someone else's. When insecurity tries to creep into your prayer life, pray anyway because you're not praying alone. Abba wants you to come to Him as your authentic self and pour your heart out to Him in prayer. Know that as you are praying, the Holy Spirit is praying on your behalf. God not only hears you; He also hears the Holy Spirit, who is praying with and for you. So, you can be confident that our Father hears your prayers and will answer according to His will. That's good news!

Personal Reflection/Application/Prayer: How has God spoken to you through today's WOTD as it relates to your life? How does today's WOTD speak to you/ your situation? What was affirmed? For what do you need to repent? What will you do differently going forward? What commitment to your spiritual growth are you going to make? Is there something that you need from God in order to live His word daily? If not for yourself, for whom do you need to pray as it relates to this WOTD? What can you thank God for and/or declare in confidence according to God's word? What can you boldly and confidently ask God for according to His word? Use the space below to record your personal revelation from God about how these verses apply to you and/or write a personal prayer to God.

day 59

Romans 8:28: **"And we know that God causes everything to work together for the good of those who love God and are called according to his purpose for them."** This is one of my absolute favorite verses. I've said it to myself and I've said it out loud. It has enabled me to persevere through challenging times with my faith intact, with hope, and with a proper perspective about situations and their outcomes. This verse is full of assurance and encouragement for those who love God and are called according to His purpose for them. That assurance and encouragement is this: There are no wasted experiences in the life of a child of God. Whether positive or negative, GOD CAUSES EVERYTHING TO WORK TOGETHER FOR OUR GOOD. The devil means harm to you in every situation, BUT GOD CAUSES IT TO WORK FOR YOUR GOOD. Not some things and not some of the time, BUT GOD CAUSES EVERYTHING - the good and the bad - that you experience in this life TO WORK FOR YOUR GOOD. The lessons that you learn from every experience - good and bad - are used by God to shape and grow you into who He destined you to be, equipping and strengthening you along the way to do the work that He put you on earth to do.[37] In addition to sunshine, rain will fall and storms will sometimes rage in your life. You will have some hurt and pain; people will turn away from you; you will have to let some people go; you will be rejected; you will experience loss; you will be confused about some things; etc..... When these times come, encourage yourself with this verse. Make it your screen saver; put it on the refrigerator and mirror. Most importantly, hide it in your heart so that you can lean on it and draw hope, strength, peace, joy, etc...during challenging times.

Personal Reflection/Application/Prayer: How has God spoken to you through today's WOTD as it relates to your life? How does today's WOTD speak to you/ your situation? What was affirmed? For what do you need to repent? What will you do differently going forward? What commitment to your spiritual growth are you going to make? Is there something that you need from God in order to live His word daily? If not for yourself, for whom do you need to pray as it relates to this

[37] Ephesians 1:11; 2:10

WOTD? What can you thank God for and/or declare in confidence according to God's word? What can you boldly and confidently ask God for according to His word? Use the space below to record your personal revelation from God about how these verses apply to you and/or write a personal prayer to God.

Romans 8:31: **"What shall we say about such wonderful things as these? If God is for us, who can ever be against us?"** Have you ever stopped to really think about the fact that God is on your side? Think about it: God gave His Son to die in your place for your sins. God put His Spirit on the inside of you as a guarantee that you belong to Him and will receive eternal life through Christ Jesus. The Holy Spirit prays for you according to God's will for your life. God causes every situation - good and bad - to work out for your good in the end. God is always on the side of His children; so, it's pointless for people to be against you. With God on your side, you are automatically in the majority and that should give you peace, confidence, joy, and determination. I encourage you to begin each day affirming that God is on your side no matter what the day holds.

Personal Reflection/Application/Prayer: How has God spoken to you through today's WOTD as it relates to your life? How does today's WOTD speak to you/ your situation? What was affirmed? For what do you need to repent? What will you do differently going forward? What commitment to your spiritual growth are you going to make? Is there something that you need from God in order to live His word daily? If not for yourself, for whom do you need to pray as it relates to this WOTD? What can you thank God for and/or declare in confidence according to God's word? What can you boldly and confidently ask God for according to His word? Use the space below to record your personal revelation from God about how these verses apply to you and/or write a personal prayer to God.

day 61

Romans 8:32-34: **"Since he did not spare even his own Son but gave him up for us all, won't he also give us everything else? Who dares accuse us whom God has chosen for his own? No one - for God himself has given us right standing with himself. Who then will condemn us? No one - for Christ Jesus died for us and was raised to life for us, and he is sitting in the place of honor at God's right hand, pleading for us."** Jesus prays for you! In v. 26-28, we learned that the Holy Spirit prays for us. Here the word of God tells us that Jesus is praying for believers as He sits at the Father's side[38]. God loves you so much that He didn't stop at sacrificing His Son so that you won't be condemned on Judgment Day. God so intends for you to win at living a life of faith in the here and now that not only does the Holy Spirit pray for you, but Jesus - the One who died so that you can win - is praying for you. God has made provision for you to have everything that you need to run this Christian race (live a life of faith) successfully and no one – absolutely no one – can condemn you if God has made you right with Himself. That, in and of itself, should give you confidence about your now and your later; it should be enough for you to make intentional choices not to compromise with this world.

Personal Reflection/Application/Prayer: How has God spoken to you through today's WOTD as it relates to your life? How does today's WOTD speak to you/ your situation? What was affirmed? For what do you need to repent? What will you do differently going forward? What commitment to your spiritual growth are you going to make? Is there something that you need from God in order to live His word daily? If not for yourself, for whom do you need to pray as it relates to this WOTD? What can you thank God for and/or declare in confidence according to God's word? What can you boldly and confidently ask God for according to His word? Use the space below to record your personal revelation from God about how these verses apply to you and/or write a personal prayer to God.

[38] Matthew 26:64; Colossians 3:1; Hebrews 12:2

day 62

Romans 8:35-37: **"Can anything ever separate us from Christ's love? Does it mean he no longer loves us if we have trouble or calamity, or are persecuted, or hungry, or destitute, or in danger, or threatened with death? (As the Scriptures say, 'For your sake we are killed every day; we are being slaughtered like sheep.') No, despite all these things, overwhelming victory is ours through Christ, who loved us."** One of the lies that the enemy speaks into our minds when we go through struggles and hard times is that God doesn't love us. Oftentimes, that lie comes in the form of the following question: "If God loves me, how can He allow all of these things to happen to me?" Well, there is no "if" God loves you. Scripture teaches that God loved you before He made the world and God loves you with an everlasting love[39]. God loved you - so much so that He gave His Son to die a criminal's death to save you before you were even born[40]. Nothing that you will ever go through in this life will cause God to not love you. In fact, God continues to show His great love for you by causing all of your struggles and hard times to work together for your good in the end[41]. Despite how bad things may seem in your life, despite how hard your struggles may be, hold tight to the truth that God loves you and has given you the victory in Jesus Christ.

Personal Reflection/Application/Prayer: How has God spoken to you through today's WOTD as it relates to your life? How does today's WOTD speak to you/ your situation? What was affirmed? For what do you need to repent? What will you do differently going forward? What commitment to your spiritual growth are you going to make? Is there something that you need from God in order to live His word daily? If not for yourself, for whom do you need to pray as it relates to this

[39] Ephesians 1:4-5; Jeremiah 31:3

[40] John 3:16

[41] Romans 8:28

WOTD? What can you thank God for and/or declare in confidence according to God's word? What can you boldly and confidently ask God for according to His word? Use the space below to record your personal revelation from God about how these verses apply to you and/or write a personal prayer to God.

day 63

Romans 8:38-39: **"And I am convinced that nothing can ever separate us from God's love. Neither death nor life, neither angels nor demons, neither our fears for today nor our worries about tomorrow - not even the powers of hell can separate us from God's love. No power in the sky above or in the earth below—indeed, nothing in all creation will ever be able to separate us from the love of God that is revealed in Christ Jesus our Lord."** God has and will always hate sin; God has and will always love you. No greater love can be shown to any of us than the love God showed for us by sacrificing His Son for our sins once and for all. Likewise, no greater love can be shown than Jesus showed by willingly laying down his life to save ours[42]. That love was given unconditionally and nothing can ever change that. No human can ever love you the way that the Father and the Son love you. It was His unconditional love for you that prompted Him to make a way for you to be reconciled to Him. Even though He left the decision to accept His love for you through Christ completely up to you, God loves you. God does not regret loving you. God's love for you prompts Him to discipline you and extend grace and mercy to you.[43] My prayer for you is the Apostle Paul's prayer: "I pray that from his glorious, unlimited resources he will empower you with inner strength through his Spirit. Then Christ will make his home in your hearts as you trust in him. Your roots will grow down into God's love and keep you strong. And may you have the power to understand, as all God's people should, how wide, how long, how high, and how deep his love is. May you experience the love of Christ, though it is too great to understand fully. Then you will be made complete with all the fullness of life and power that comes from God."[44] Think about how much God loves you as you go throughout today and begin each day from now on reflecting on the reality that nothing - no thing - will ever cause God to not love you.

---

[42] John 10:11, 17-18; John 15:13; Hebrews 10:1-14; 1 John 3:16

[43] Proverbs 3:12; Hebrews 12:4-11

[44] Ephesians 3:16-19

Personal Reflection/Application/Prayer: How has God spoken to you through today's WOTD as it relates to your life? How does today's WOTD speak to you/ your situation? What was affirmed? For what do you need to repent? What will you do differently going forward? What commitment to your spiritual growth are you going to make? Is there something that you need from God in order to live His word daily? If not for yourself, for whom do you need to pray as it relates to this WOTD? What can you thank God for and/or declare in confidence according to God's word? What can you boldly and confidently ask God for according to His word? Use the space below to record your personal revelation from God about how these verses apply to you and/or write a personal prayer to God.

day 64

Romans 9:15-16**: "For God said to Moses, 'I will show mercy to anyone I choose, and I will show compassion to anyone I choose.' So it is God who decides to show mercy. We can neither choose it nor work for it."** Have you ever felt that someone didn't deserve a benefit, chance, position, etc... that they received? Have you ever questioned God as to why someone didn't get what you felt they deserved or why someone received something you felt that they didn't deserve? (Have you considered that someone may have had those same feelings/questions when you received God's mercy and compassion?) I sure have; that is, until I truly accepted God's sovereignty and understood that everything that happens in this life, whether good or bad, is being used by God as a part of His master plan. Even though we may not understand God's reasons, God doesn't make arbitrary decisions; He is intentional in all that He does. He decides to whom He will show mercy and compassion and that decision has nothing to do with us. He, and He alone, decides whom He is going to use and how He is going to use them to advance Kingdom purpose.

Personal Reflection/Application/Prayer: How has God spoken to you through today's WOTD as it relates to your life? How does today's WOTD speak to you/ your situation? What was affirmed? For what do you need to repent? What will you do differently going forward? What commitment to your spiritual growth are you going to make? Is there something that you need from God in order to live His word daily? If not for yourself, for whom do you need to pray as it relates to this WOTD? What can you thank God for and/or declare in confidence according to God's word? What can you boldly and confidently ask God for according to His word? Use the space below to record your personal revelation from God about how these verses apply to you and/or write a personal prayer to God.

day 65

Romans 9:20-21: **"No, don't say that. Who are you, a mere human being, to argue with God? Should the thing that was created say to the one who created it, 'Why have you made me like this?' When a potter makes jars out of clay, doesn't he have the right to use the same lump of clay to make one jar for decoration and another to throw garbage into?"** WOW! Clay has many uses, which makes it so valuable; however, clay doesn't know how it's needed. It doesn't know what it's needed to be and do; it can't demand to be made into anything. A potter, on the other hand, has vision and creativity and specializes in transforming common lumps of clay into intentional custom-made works of art that have a unique purpose. Imagine the potential in that common lump of clay that is full of possibilities in the potter's hand. I can hear the clay excitedly asking the potter, "*What will you make me into?*" I can hear the clay saying to the potter, "*I can't wait to see what you transform me into!*" "*Wow! I am beautiful work of art! Show me my purpose so that I can be the best that you created me to be.*" Beloved, you are the lump of clay and God is the potter. God created you for His purpose; He was not created for yours. The only reason you are alive is because God purposed your life. As such, you don't have a right to devalue yourself nor complain to God about how He made you; especially, since your purpose doesn't come from you. Instead of fault-finding, I encourage you to approach God like an excited lump of clay. Ask your Creator, "*What will You make me into?*" Say to your Creator, "*I can't wait to see what you transform me into!*" "*Wow! I am beautiful! Show me my purpose so that I can be the best that you created me to be.*"

Personal Reflection/Application/Prayer: How has God spoken to you through today's WOTD as it relates to your life? How does today's WOTD speak to you/your situation? What was affirmed? For what do you need to repent? What will you do differently going forward? What commitment to your spiritual growth are you going to make? Is there something that you need from God in order to live His word daily? If not for yourself, for whom do you need to pray as it relates to this

WOTD? What can you thank God for and/or declare in confidence according to God's word? What can you boldly and confidently ask God for according to His word? Use the space below to record your personal revelation from God about how these verses apply to you and/or write a personal prayer to God.

day 66

Romans 9:30-32: **"What does all this mean? Even though the Gentiles were not trying to follow God's standards, they were made right with God. And it was by faith that this took place. But the people of Israel, who tried so hard to get right with God by keeping the law, never succeeded. Why not? Because they were trying to get right with God by keeping the law instead of by trusting in him. They stumbled over the great rock in their path."** These verses are a clear example of the difference between "relationship" and "religion". Like the people of Israel, religious people believe that strictly following rules sets them apart and makes them right in God's eyes. They believe in God with their heads, which is why Jesus was a stumbling block in their path. The Gentiles, on the other hand, believed in God with their hearts. They trusted God's word and put their faith in Jesus Christ, which made them - and makes us - right with God. Their heart relationship with God caused them to trust God's standards for living. They were compelled to live godly lives not by rules, but by God's love for them and their love for Him in return. What about you? Do you have a head or heart relationship with the Father? What compels you to live a godly life: rules or faith? Is Jesus a stumbling block (the great rock) in your path? If so, why?

Personal Reflection/Application/Prayer: How has God spoken to you through today's WOTD as it relates to your life? How does today's WOTD speak to you/ your situation? What was affirmed? For what do you need to repent? What will you do differently going forward? What commitment to your spiritual growth are you going to make? Is there something that you need from God in order to live His word daily? If not for yourself, for whom do you need to pray as it relates to this WOTD? What can you thank God for and/or declare in confidence according to God's word? What can you boldly and confidently ask God for according to His word? Use the space below to record your personal revelation from God about how these verses apply to you and/or write a personal prayer to God.

day 67

Romans 10:2-4: **"I know what enthusiasm they [people of Israel] have for God, but it is misdirected zeal. For they don't understand God's way of making people right with himself. Refusing to accept God's way, they cling to their own way of getting right with God by trying to keep the law. For Christ has already accomplished the purpose for which the law was given. As a result, all who believe in him are made right with God."** JESUS DID IT! Salvation is the act of being saved from the penalty of sin; it is the only means by which we can be in relationship with God. Salvation is the adoption process into God's family; it is how we become His children. Salvation is HOW you are made right with God; it is the beginning of your relationship with God.. No matter how many "right" things you do, you CANNOT make yourself right with God. Your actions, alone, CANNOT save you. How do you get right with God? Believe in what Jesus HAS ALREADY ACCOMPLISHED on your behalf. That, and that alone, is how God makes people right with Himself. With all of the false teaching in our world today, make it your mission to know and live the truth. Share this Good News with everyone you know so that there is no doubt in their minds about how to get right with God. JESUS DID IT! TRUST AND BELIEVE IT!

Personal Reflection/Application/Prayer: How has God spoken to you through today's WOTD as it relates to your life? How does today's WOTD speak to you/ your situation? What was affirmed? For what do you need to repent? What will you do differently going forward? What commitment to your spiritual growth are you going to make? Is there something that you need from God in order to live His word daily? If not for yourself, for whom do you need to pray as it relates to this WOTD? What can you thank God for and/or declare in confidence according to God's word? What can you boldly and confidently ask God for according to His word? Use the space below to record your personal revelation from God about how these verses apply to you and/or write a personal prayer to God.

day 68

Romans 10:9-10: **"If you confess with your mouth that Jesus is Lord and believe in your heart that God raised him from the dead, you will be saved. For it is by believing in your heart that you are made right with God, and it is by confessing with your mouth that you are saved."** AND is a coordinating conjunction, which means that what comes before and after it go together. These verses make it clear that salvation is a two-step process that involves both an internal decision and an external act: belief AND confession. Empty confessions/simply uttering the words out of your mouth because someone tells you to repeat after them is worthless unless you actually believe those words are true. You must both BELIEVE in your heart that God raised Jesus from the dead (internal decision) AND CONFESS (speak the words out of your mouth) that Jesus is Lord (external act). Your belief is what makes you righteous AND your confession is what saves you. Thank God that salvation isn't dependent upon strict adherence to the law because not one of us would be saved. Thank God that salvation is dependent upon our faith in and confession of Jesus Christ as Lord. Thank God that salvation can happen anywhere and at any time: home, parking lot, store, office, over the phone, etc.... This Good News is too good to keep to yourself. There is no better time than now to tell those whom you know who aren't in a relationship with the Father how they can inherit eternal life. I believe that sharing the Good News is the greatest act of love that we can show those around us.

Personal Reflection/Application/Prayer: How has God spoken to you through today's WOTD as it relates to your life? How does today's WOTD speak to you/your situation? What was affirmed? For what do you need to repent? What will you do differently going forward? What commitment to your spiritual growth are you going to make? Is there something that you need from God in order to live His word daily? If not for yourself, for whom do you need to pray as it relates to this WOTD? What can you thank God for and/or declare in confidence according to God's word? What can you boldly and confidently ask God for according to His word? Use the space below to record your personal revelation from God about how these verses apply to you and/or write a personal prayer to God.

day 69

Romans 10:11-13: **"As the Scriptures tell us, 'Anyone who trusts in him will never be disgraced.' Jew and Gentile are the same in this respect. They have the same Lord, who gives generously to all who call on him. For 'Everyone who calls on the name of the Lord will be saved.'"** Faith in Jesus, demonstrated by believing in your heart and confessing with your mouth, is the only qualifier for salvation. In our world, man has created so many disqualifiers to deny people access to what they deem the good life/prestige. Whether the access is to schools, jobs, clubs/organizations, VIP sections, etc., your last name, socio-economic status, appearance, education, race (which is a man-made concept), etc., can be used by others to either grant or deny you access. I'm so glad that no human being can set qualifications for salvation; otherwise, both you and I would more than likely not have measured up to man's standard. Becoming a member of God's family is the most important membership decision that anyone can make and it trumps any other membership we have, even family. God, and God alone, set the qualifications for membership in His family and it applies to "Anyone" and "Everyone": belief in and confession of Jesus Christ as Lord. That includes me and I'm so glad that I will never be disgraced. What about you?

Personal Reflection/Application/Prayer: How has God spoken to you through today's WOTD as it relates to your life? How does today's WOTD speak to you/your situation? What was affirmed? For what do you need to repent? What will you do differently going forward? What commitment to your spiritual growth are you going to make? Is there something that you need from God in order to live His word daily? If not for yourself, for whom do you need to pray as it relates to this WOTD? What can you thank God for and/or declare in confidence according to God's word? What can you boldly and confidently ask God for according to His word? Use the space below to record your personal revelation from God about how these verses apply to you and/or write a personal prayer to God.

day 70

Romans 10:14-15, 17: **"But how can they call on him to save them unless they believe in him? And how can they believe in him if they have never heard about him? And how can they hear about him unless someone tells them? And how will anyone go and tell them without being sent? That is why the Scriptures say, 'How beautiful are the feet of messengers who bring good news!'...So faith comes from hearing, that is, hearing the Good News about Christ.'"** In order for anyone to put their faith in Christ, someone must tell them the Good News about Christ. The Bible describes the feet of those who bring good news as beautiful. How beautiful are your feet when it comes to telling the unsaved about Christ?

Personal Reflection/Application/Prayer: How has God spoken to you through today's WOTD as it relates to your life? How does today's WOTD speak to you/your situation? What was affirmed? For what do you need to repent? What will you do differently going forward? What commitment to your spiritual growth are you going to make? Is there something that you need from God in order to live His word daily? If not for yourself, for whom do you need to pray as it relates to this WOTD? What can you thank God for and/or declare in confidence according to God's word? What can you boldly and confidently ask God for according to His word? Use the space below to record your personal revelation from God about how these verses apply to you and/or write a personal prayer to God.

day 71

Romans 11:29: **"For God's gifts and his call can never be withdrawn."** Even though the people of Israel rejected Christ and rebelled against God, God still loved them. They were His chosen people as a result of His covenant with their ancestors Abraham, Isaac, and Jacob[45]. Because of this covenant, God always preserved a remnant of Israel who remained faithful. God ALWAYS keeps His word. Whatever God has spoken is and will be. Whatever gifts God gives a person by His Spirit will not be taken away. This encourages me; especially, when I think about those whom I know personally who are in a rebellious place. God still loves them and didn't take back the spiritual gifts He gave them by His Spirit. Their lives have value and I am hopeful as I pray for them that they will turn back to God and be restored; that their gifts will be used to advance the Kingdom of God. This verse is also a reminder for me of the investment that God made in me and my responsibility to use my gifts and the calling on my life to His glory. I am truly grateful and I don't want to squander God's investment in me. What about you?

Personal Reflection/Application/Prayer: How has God spoken to you through today's WOTD as it relates to your life? How does today's WOTD speak to you/ your situation? What was affirmed? For what do you need to repent? What will you do differently going forward? What commitment to your spiritual growth are you going to make? Is there something that you need from God in order to live His word daily? If not for yourself, for whom do you need to pray as it relates to this WOTD? What can you thank God for and/or declare in confidence according to God's word? What can you boldly and confidently ask God for according to His word? Use the space below to record your personal revelation from God about how these verses apply to you and/or write a personal prayer to God.

[45] Exodus 32:13; Acts 3:13

day 72

Romans 11:33-36: **"Oh, how great are God's riches and wisdom and knowledge! How impossible it is for us to understand his decisions and his ways! For who can know the LORD'S thoughts? Who knows enough to give him advice? And who has given him so much that he needs to pay it back? For everything comes from him and exists by his power and is intended for his glory. All glory to him forever! Amen."** How many times have you honestly questioned God - why He allowed some things to happen, why He didn't allow those things that you wanted to happen? How many times have you acted as if you knew better than God what you needed? How many times have you felt, acted, and/or spoken as if God owed you something? God is omniscient, omnipotent, and omnipresent. I AM is too big to be boxed in by our limited understanding of who I AM is.[46] There are some things that we will never understand or be able to rationalize or fully explain when it comes to why and how God does what God does. His ways and thoughts are higher than we can comprehend.[47] God doesn't owe any of us anything and not one of us, no matter how educated we are, can tell God how to be God. Not one of us knows better than God what is right and wrong or what is best for us. God is the source of all creation and everything that God created was created on purpose for His divine purpose. God's divine purpose is to get the glory out of all that God created, including you/your life.

Personal Reflection/Application/Prayer: How has God spoken to you through today's WOTD as it relates to your life? How does today's WOTD speak to you/ your situation? What was affirmed? For what do you need to repent? What will you do differently going forward? What commitment to your spiritual growth are you going to make? Is there something that you need from God in order to live His word daily? If not for yourself, for whom do you need to pray as it relates to this

[46] Exodus 3:14

[47] Isaiah 55:8-9

WOTD? What can you thank God for and/or declare in confidence according to God's word? What can you boldly and confidently ask God for according to His word? Use the space below to record your personal revelation from God about how these verses apply to you and/or write a personal prayer to God.

day 73

Romans 12:1: **"And so, dear brothers and sisters, I plead with you to give your bodies to God because of all he has done for you. Let them be a living and holy sacrifice—the kind he will find acceptable. This is truly the way to worship him."** What has God done for you and what should you do for God in return? By sending Jesus to die in our place for our sins, God made it possible for us to be saved and have a relationship with Him. Your life is NOT yours to do as you please. Your freedom cost Jesus His life – a life that He willingly gave up. In return for God's gift of salvation, you and I have a responsibility to give ALL of ourselves - mind, body, and spirit - to God. In Christ, we have been set apart from the world and the sacrifice we give is refusing to live according to the world's ways. Telling ourselves "no" when our flesh is tempted to disobey God is how we are living and holy sacrifices that please God. It's how we worship Him. Our lifestyle is to be an act of worship. Worship isn't where we go; rather, it's what we do. Think about it: Every decision you make to live for God daily is an act of worship. Every time you tell the truth when you are tempted to lie, it's worship. Every time you extend yourself to help others/put others before you put yourself, it's worship. On the flip side, consider the lack of gratitude/appreciation that you show God when you ignore the Holy Spirit's leading and/or when you do what you want to do instead of what God wants you to do. Determine from this day forward to give ALL of you, including your emotions, to our Father in heaven. Every time you refrain from making an emotional response to people/situations and instead, ask the Holy Spirit to lead you: worship. All of you also includes your heart. Every time you put aside selfish motives and act honorably: worship. Every time you put forth your best effort at work, school, serving in ministry, cleaning, taking care of the things God has blessed you with, etc.…: worship. Every time you express gratitude instead of complaints: worship. Determine to be a living and holy sacrifice for him. Determine to live a life of worship because of ALL God has done for you.

Personal Reflection/Application/Prayer: How has God spoken to you through today's WOTD as it relates to your life? How does today's WOTD speak to you/ your situation? What was affirmed? For what do you need to repent? What will you do differently going forward? What commitment to your spiritual growth are you going to make? Is there something that you need from God in order to live His word daily? If not for yourself, for whom do you need to pray as it relates to this WOTD? What can you thank God for and/or declare in confidence according to God's word? What can you boldly and confidently ask God for according to His word? Use the space below to record your personal revelation from God about how these verses apply to you and/or write a personal prayer to God.

day 74

Romans 12:2: **"Don't copy the behavior and customs of this world, but let God transform you into a new person by changing the way you think. Then you will learn to know God's will for you, which is good and pleasing and perfect."** The world's way of living is always hostile to God, always rebelling against God by living according to its sinful nature.[48] Christians are not supposed to live like the world, like those who are not God's children. While there should be a clear distinction between Christians and people who aren't, it doesn't happen on its own. That's why there are so many carnally-minded Christians whose witness for Christ is corrupted. They are saved; yet, they live as if they are not. God will never force His way on you. You, as a child of God, must surrender your sinful nature/your worldly way of thinking to God.[49] You must "let" God transform your way of thinking if your actions are going to show that you belong to Him. It's the only way for you to learn God's good, pleasing, and perfect will for you. Letting the Holy Spirit control your thinking "leads to life and peace" according to God's word.[50] Question: Have you fully surrendered your sinful nature to God? If not, why not; especially, since living by it leads to death? What are you gaining from the world that will benefit you more than God's good, pleasing, and perfect will for your life? If you no longer live by your sinful nature, how are you praying for those who are? How are you interacting with them? What example are you setting for them? Are you like honey - drawing them to God by your example or are you like ammonia - repelling them from God?

Personal Reflection/Application/Prayer: How has God spoken to you through today's WOTD as it relates to your life? How does today's WOTD speak to you/your situation? What was affirmed? For what do you need to repent? What will you do differently going forward? What commitment to your spiritual growth are you going to make? Is there something that you need from God in order to live His word daily? If not for yourself, for whom do you need to pray as it relates to this

---

[48] Romans 8:7

[49] Romans 8:5

[50] Romans 8:6

WOTD? What can you thank God for and/or declare in confidence according to God's word? What can you boldly and confidently ask God for according to His word? Use the space below to record your personal revelation from God about how these verses apply to you and/or write a personal prayer to God.

day 75

Romans 12:3: "**...Don't think you are better than you really are. Be honest in your evaluation of yourselves, measuring yourselves by the faith God has given us.**" Do you know people who act like they are better than others? Do you know people who embellish their abilities? This verse calls us to check ourselves. No one is good at everything. Having an inflated self-perception gets in the way of our effectiveness for the Kingdom; it becomes a barrier to us working in unity with others. We must be honest with ourselves about our strengths and weaknesses and trust God to work within us to accomplish His purposes for our lives according to His standards. How honest are you with yourself about you? By whose standard have you been evaluating yourself: yours or God's?

Personal Reflection/Application/Prayer: How has God spoken to you through today's WOTD as it relates to your life? How does today's WOTD speak to you/ your situation? What was affirmed? For what do you need to repent? What will you do differently going forward? What commitment to your spiritual growth are you going to make? Is there something that you need from God in order to live His word daily? If not for yourself, for whom do you need to pray as it relates to this WOTD? What can you thank God for and/or declare in confidence according to God's word? What can you boldly and confidently ask God for according to His word? Use the space below to record your personal revelation from God about how these verses apply to you and/or write a personal prayer to God.

day 76

Romans 12:4-5: **"Just as our bodies have many parts and each part has a special function, so it is with Christ's body. We are many parts of one body, and we all belong to each other."** In the Kingdom of God, EVERY Christian has a special role to fulfill in the overall health and productivity of the body of Christ. That's why every Christian should be serving in God's church and should be valued for his/her contribution. There are needs to be met in the church and in our communities that require us to work together in the church if the church is going to be able to meet those needs. Have you considered the fact that God has given you a special function in the body of Christ? Have you considered that YOUR active presence AND participation are crucial to the church's ability to meet those needs? Have you considered the impact of you not serving in God's Kingdom? If not, think about these things.

Personal Reflection/Application/Prayer: How has God spoken to you through today's WOTD as it relates to your life? How does today's WOTD speak to you/ your situation? What was affirmed? For what do you need to repent? What will you do differently going forward? What commitment to your spiritual growth are you going to make? Is there something that you need from God in order to live His word daily? If not for yourself, for whom do you need to pray as it relates to this WOTD? What can you thank God for and/or declare in confidence according to God's word? What can you boldly and confidently ask God for according to His word? Use the space below to record your personal revelation from God about how these verses apply to you and/or write a personal prayer to God.

day 77

Romans 12:6-8: **"In his grace, God has given us different gifts for doing certain things well. So if God has given you the ability to prophesy, speak out with as much faith as God has given you. If your gift is serving others, serve them well. If you are a teacher, teach well. If your gift is encouraging others, be encouraging. If it is giving, give generously. If God has given you leadership ability, take the responsibility seriously. And if you have a gift for showing kindness to others, do it gladly."** Through the Holy Spirit, God has given EVERY believer at least one spiritual gift to use in Kingdom service.[51] Whatever your gift is, the expectation is that you use it to the best of your ability. Your gift is a part of you, is with you wherever you are, and is to be used wherever you are to God's glory. You'll find that using your gift(s) isn't a forced experience. It comes naturally and gives you a sense of purpose and fulfillment beyond measure. Do you know what your gift(s) is/are? If so, are you using your gifts in Kingdom service? Do you also find yourself using those same skills in your profession and/or in your social/organizational circles? If you don't know what your spiritual gifts are, I highly encourage you to take a spiritual gifts assessment. If you know what your gifts are, but are not using them in Kingdom service, you are being disobedient to God. In either case, you're ineffective in Kingdom service and that is not God's will for you.

Personal Reflection/Application/Prayer: How has God spoken to you through today's WOTD as it relates to your life? How does today's WOTD speak to you/ your situation? What was affirmed? For what do you need to repent? What will you do differently going forward? What commitment to your spiritual growth are you going to make? Is there something that you need from God in order to live His word daily? If not for yourself, for whom do you need to pray as it relates to this WOTD? What can you thank God for and/or declare in confidence according to God's word? What can you boldly and confidently ask God for according to His word? Use the space below to record your personal revelation from God about how these verses apply to you and/or write a personal prayer to God.

[51] 1 Corinthians 12:7, 11

day 78

Romans 12:9-10: **"Don't just pretend to love others. Really love them. Hate what is wrong. Hold tightly to what is good. Love each other with genuine affection, and take delight in honoring each other."** Love, as used in these verses, is the genuine love that should exist among family (parents to children, children to parents, sibling to sibling). The body of Christ is a family and we are to genuinely love each other, helping each other to become better people. We should genuinely respect and value each other. This love goes beyond being courteous and polite. It is demonstrated by giving of our time, effort, and finances. It is demonstrated by our active participation in each other's lives. As the body of Christ, we are to collectively extend this same love in our communities. Questions for your consideration: How genuine is your love walk with fellow believers, not just the ones you prefer to associate with? How genuine is the love walk of your local faith community towards those in the community; especially, those who are unbelievers? Does your love walk set you apart from others as true representatives of Christ's church? Pray for the body of Christ to be true representatives of God's love in the communities where God has planted us.

Personal Reflection/Application/Prayer: How has God spoken to you through today's WOTD as it relates to your life? How does today's WOTD speak to you/ your situation? What was affirmed? For what do you need to repent? What will you do differently going forward? What commitment to your spiritual growth are you going to make? Is there something that you need from God in order to live His word daily? If not for yourself, for whom do you need to pray as it relates to this WOTD? What can you thank God for and/or declare in confidence according to God's word? What can you boldly and confidently ask God for according to His word? Use the space below to record your personal revelation from God about how these verses apply to you and/or write a personal prayer to God.

day 79

Romans 12:11-12: **"Never be lazy, but work hard and serve the Lord enthusiastically. Rejoice in confident hope. Be patient in trouble, and keep on praying."** Lazy people dread doing anything, even if it's for their good in the end, and tend to do just enough to be able to technically say that they did something. Christians are to be passionate and hardworking when it comes to living our faith. Everything that we do, we do for the Lord because of our faith. God's word is true, and His word will come to pass. Because of this, we can live with confident expectation (hope) no matter what we encounter in this life. We can be patient when going through trials and tribulations because we know that God is working for our good in the midst of them. Lastly, we are reminded to always go to God in prayer: to let Him know how much we love and adore Him, to confess our sins, to thank Him for what He has done for us, to listen to what He has to say to us, and to ask Him for what we need. All of these instructions: work hard, serve enthusiastically, rejoice confidently, be patient, and keep praying are to be a part of our daily lives. Imagine what transformation would happen in our personal lives if we committed to consistently obeying these simple instructions daily. Imagine its impact in the body of Christ collectively and in our communities.

Personal Reflection/Application/Prayer: How has God spoken to you through today's WOTD as it relates to your life? How does today's WOTD speak to you/your situation? What was affirmed? For what do you need to repent? What will you do differently going forward? What commitment to your spiritual growth are you going to make? Is there something that you need from God in order to live His word daily? If not for yourself, for whom do you need to pray as it relates to this WOTD? What can you thank God for and/or declare in confidence according to God's word? What can you boldly and confidently ask God for according to His word? Use the space below to record your personal revelation from God about how these verses apply to you and/or write a personal prayer to God.

day 80

Romans 12:13: **"When God's people are in need, be ready to help them. Always be eager to practice hospitality."** As a community of faith, Christians are supposed to help meet each other's needs. We are supposed to be here for each other because we are family. Jesus made that plain in Matthew 12:50 when he told the crowd that those who obey God are his true family members. The early church in Acts set the perfect example of how we are to be here for one another, helping in times of need and showing hospitality towards each other.[52] How willing are you to help your brothers and sisters in Christ; especially, if helping involves you giving your money, property, and/or possessions? How willing are you to be inconvenienced to help your brothers and sisters in Christ? How hospitable are you towards others? How eager are you to open your home to God's people for fellowship and sharing meals together? Can you imagine how extending ourselves in this way would enable us to strengthen each other and win souls to Christ by how they see us treat each other? I challenge you to be intentional about (1) looking for ways to help meet a practical need of your brothers and sisters in Christ - and not only those with whom you are personally comfortable and (2) practicing hospitality beyond your personal circle of comfort.

Personal Reflection/Application/Prayer: How has God spoken to you through today's WOTD as it relates to your life? How does today's WOTD speak to you/ your situation? What was affirmed? For what do you need to repent? What will you do differently going forward? What commitment to your spiritual growth are you going to make? Is there something that you need from God in order to live His word daily? If not for yourself, for whom do you need to pray as it relates to this WOTD? What can you thank God for and/or declare in confidence according to God's word? What can you boldly and confidently ask God for according to His word? Use the space below to record your personal revelation from God about how these verses apply to you and/or write a personal prayer to God.

---

[52] Acts 2:44-47

day 81

Romans 12:14: **"Bless those who persecute you. Don't curse them; pray that God will bless them."** This one here can be hard to do. Why would God expect us to show love to our enemies? The answer to this question is found in Matthew 5:45-48. After telling the crowds to love and pray for their enemies, Jesus explains that doing this shows that we're true children of God. If we only love and pray for those whom we love, we're no different from those who don't follow Christ. Being kind to those who are unkind to us is not something that we can do in our own strength. It takes true AND DAILY submission to and reliance on the Holy Spirit. As we grow and mature in our faith, we become more and more like Christ and can GENUINELY repay evil with good and pray for those who wrong us because doing God's will is more important to us than doing our own. Question: How are you doing in this area of your Christian walk? Be honest with yourself. God already knows because He sees your actions, hears your words, and knows your thoughts. If this is an area of growth for you, ask God to help you by His Spirit; then, do what the Spirit says. It won't be easy at first because your initial response is tied to your emotions, but ask the Holy Spirit to empower you. Each step you take to grow and mature in this area of your Christian walk makes the next step easier until it becomes a natural part of you. You won't even spend time mulling over the offense because your focus will be on glorifying God.

Personal Reflection/Application/Prayer: How has God spoken to you through today's WOTD as it relates to your life? How does today's WOTD speak to you/ your situation? What was affirmed? For what do you need to repent? What will you do differently going forward? What commitment to your spiritual growth are you going to make? Is there something that you need from God in order to live His word daily? If not for yourself, for whom do you need to pray as it relates to this WOTD? What can you thank God for and/or declare in confidence according to God's word? What can you boldly and confidently ask God for according to His word? Use the space below to record your personal revelation from God about how these verses apply to you and/or write a personal prayer to God.

day 82

Romans 12:15: **"Be happy with those who are happy, and weep with those who weep."** Have you ever known people who can't be happy for others, who rain on others' parades, or who are insensitive to those who are going through rough times? I have. If the focus isn't on them, they aren't interested. If they aren't happy, they don't want others to be happy. This verse is a gentle reminder that our lives aren't just about us and what we want. We live in community others and should share in each other's lives. As Christians, we are to genuinely celebrate with others when they are happy. Likewise, we are to empathize (put ourselves in another's shoes and feel what they feel), not just sympathize (feel sorry for another), with others when they are going through a rough time. Living this verse helps to strengthen the bonds of community and enables us to be the example God expects us to be for the world. Self-check: Are you genuinely happy with others even if things aren't going the way you want them to for you? Have you ever cried with someone because of what they were going through? Both of these actions require you to remove yourself from a place of self-focus and become others-focused. If these are areas of growth for you, ask God to reveal to you the root of your inability to do either or both. Then, ask Him to shift your focus from self to others so that you can best represent Him in community with others. If neither of these areas is challenging for you, keep letting your light shine for the Kingdom and pray for those who are challenged to live this verse.

Personal Reflection/Application/Prayer: How has God spoken to you through today's WOTD as it relates to your life? How does today's WOTD speak to you/your situation? What was affirmed? For what do you need to repent? What will you do differently going forward? What commitment to your spiritual growth are you going to make? Is there something that you need from God in order to live His word daily? If not for yourself, for whom do you need to pray as it relates to this WOTD? What can you thank God for and/or declare in confidence according to God's word? What can you boldly and confidently ask God for according to His word? Use the space below to record your personal revelation from God about how these verses apply to you and/or write a personal prayer to God.

day 83

Romans 12:16: **"Live in harmony with each other. Don't be too proud to enjoy the company of ordinary people. And don't think you know it all!"** These three commands concern how we interact with/treat each other. (1) While we are not all alike and are not expected to do things robotically, as Christians, we are to be like-minded in our focus/purpose and that focus/purpose is to do God's will. The early church described in Acts 4:32-35 gives us an example of what being united in heart and mind looks like. (2) Arrogance and thinking that others are beneath us is not pleasing to God, nor is thinking that we're too good to do seemingly menial tasks or interact with people who are different from us. Remember, falling from our high horse comes as a result of self-exaltation.[53] (3) You don't know everything. Not one of us does. Admit that fact to yourself right now. Refuse to be the type of person who won't listen to those who know more/better than you about anything. Many a person has gotten caught up and forfeited opportunities because they refused to listen to those who attempted to provide godly instruction and wisdom. Self-check: How harmoniously are you living with other believers? Is your focus in life on living God's will or your own? How well do you collaborate with other believers? Are you a source of discord and confusion? Do you think that you are better than others? Do you look down on others? How, if at all, do you interact with those who are different from you? Are you haughty (prideful) or humble? Are you the smartest person you know? How easy is it for you to own the fact that you don't know everything? How easy is it for you to accept and apply godly instruction and wisdom from others and not just the people you like? Be honest with yourself about where you are in each of these areas. Any attitude or action contrary to God's will for your life as His child is a stumbling block for you and others. While you may be readily able to recognize external stumbling blocks in these areas, internal stumbling blocks are most dangerous because you tend to not see your own. Pray for yourself and others, asking God to remove any stumbling blocks that prevent you from living your best life for Him.

[53] Proverbs 16:18

Personal Reflection/Application/Prayer: How has God spoken to you through today's WOTD as it relates to your life? How does today's WOTD speak to you/ your situation? What was affirmed? For what do you need to repent? What will you do differently going forward? What commitment to your spiritual growth are you going to make? Is there something that you need from God in order to live His word daily? If not for yourself, for whom do you need to pray as it relates to this WOTD? What can you thank God for and/or declare in confidence according to God's word? What can you boldly and confidently ask God for according to His word? Use the space below to record your personal revelation from God about how these verses apply to you and/or write a personal prayer to God.

day 84

Romans 12:17-18: **"Never pay back evil with more evil. Do things in such a way that everyone can see you are honorable. Do all that you can to live in peace with everyone."** The influence of this world says, "If you get me; then, I'm going to get you back." That's revenge. To intentionally plan to harm someone in any way, regardless of the reason, is evil and not of God. When we pay people back for wronging us, we allow our emotions to dictate our actions. When our emotions are in control of us, it means that the devil is in control of us. As children of God, we are to take our hurt and anger to Him and allow the Holy Spirit to process us through it so that we can respond in a manner that pleases God. This can be hard to do; but as we put God's will over our own, the Holy Spirit will enable us to resist the temptation to seek revenge and seek to live at peace with others. Please understand: Living an honorable and peaceful life ≠ letting people run over top of you and treat you any kind of way. Understand also that reconciliation takes more than you. You are responsible for *trying* to make peace with others; you have no control over whether they are willing to do likewise. Your Father in Heaven has already said that He will take care of anyone who wrongs you how He sees fit and when He sees fit.[54] Since God cannot lie, you can trust Him at His word; so, focus your efforts on living an honorable life for His glory.

Personal Reflection/Application/Prayer: How has God spoken to you through today's WOTD as it relates to your life? How does today's WOTD speak to you/ your situation? What was affirmed? For what do you need to repent? What will you do differently going forward? What commitment to your spiritual growth are you going to make? Is there something that you need from God in order to live His word daily? If not for yourself, for whom do you need to pray as it relates to this WOTD? What can you thank God for and/or declare in confidence according to God's word? What can you boldly and confidently ask God for according to His word? Use the space below to record your personal revelation from God about how these verses apply to you and/or write a personal prayer to God.

---

[54] Romans 12:19

day 85

Romans 12:19-20: **"Dear friends, never take revenge. Leave that to the righteous anger of God. For the Scriptures say, 'I will take revenge; I will pay them back,' says the LORD. Instead, 'If your enemies are hungry, feed them. If they are thirsty, give them something to drink. In doing this, you will heap burning coals of shame on their heads.'"** People who mistreat God's children have absolutely no clue what they have coming to them. Same as with yesterday's WOTD, we are told matter-of-factly not to take revenge against people. Doing so is rooted in evil. Abba, our Daddy, has told us that revenge is for Him to do, not us. Unlike our anger, God's anger is righteous. He, not us, is always right and justified in paying back those who do evil. (Side note: If we truly understood that our sin is just cause for God to display His righteous anger towards us, we would appreciate His grace and Jesus' sacrifice to save us all from it all the more and endeavor to live lives that reflect our appreciation.) Planning and taking revenge on others requires a lot of energy, and negative energy at that. Instead, we are to meet their needs if we have the means to do so, as well as be hospitable and nice to them. This requires true submission to God and humility in front of people who more than likely won't appreciate your acts of kindness. (I can say that because I've had to do it and it wasn't appreciated. It was actually mocked.) Truthfully, extending yourself to them isn't about them; it's about you trusting and obeying God. Look at what happens when we take the high road: Being kind to our enemies despite their treatment of us shames them because every act of our kindness makes their sin more apparent to them to the point where it overwhelms their conscience. The weight of that shame is compared to someone piling hot coals on top of their heads. That's just the impact of our obedience to God on them. On top of that, they have God's righteous anger coming their way. That's why we must pray for people who mistreat us. Again, they have absolutely no clue what they are doing to themselves by wronging us. Remember, taking revenge is for God to do; trusting and obeying God is for you to do.

Personal Reflection/Application/Prayer: How has God spoken to you through today's WOTD as it relates to your life? How does today's WOTD speak to you/ your situation? What was affirmed? For what do you need to repent? What will you do differently going forward? What commitment to your spiritual growth are you going to make? Is there something that you need from God in order to live His word daily? If not for yourself, for whom do you need to pray as it relates to this WOTD? What can you thank God for and/or declare in confidence according to God's word? What can you boldly and confidently ask God for according to His word? Use the space below to record your personal revelation from God about how these verses apply to you and/or write a personal prayer to God.

day 86

Romans 12:21: **"Don't let evil conquer you, but conquer evil by doing good."** If you take revenge against someone, evil has conquered you. The way for you to get the victory over evil is to do good to others, including those who have done evil to you. You can't genuinely do good unless you intentionally choose to walk in forgiveness. Remember, forgiveness isn't about whether the person deserves it because they probably don't (just like you didn't deserve for God to forgive you). Forgiveness keeps your heart from becoming hard so that you can do good even when evil has been done to you. Did you know that there are benefits to choosing to do good over taking revenge that you may not have even realized? Choosing to do good to someone who has wronged you may not only make them ashamed of how they treated you; it may also lead them to repent and come into relationship with Christ. Even if they don't, your conscience will be clear and you will be blameless before God. What an amazing witness for the Kingdom of God!

Personal Reflection/Application/Prayer: How has God spoken to you through today's WOTD as it relates to your life? How does today's WOTD speak to you/your situation? What was affirmed? For what do you need to repent? What will you do differently going forward? What commitment to your spiritual growth are you going to make? Is there something that you need from God in order to live His word daily? If not for yourself, for whom do you need to pray as it relates to this WOTD? What can you thank God for and/or declare in confidence according to God's word? What can you boldly and confidently ask God for according to His word? Use the space below to record your personal revelation from God about how these verses apply to you and/or write a personal prayer to God.

day 87

Romans 13:1-2: **"Everyone must submit to governing authorities. For all authority comes from God, and those in positions of authority have been placed there by God. So anyone who rebels against authority is rebelling against what God has instituted, and they will be punished."** 1 Samuel 8 details how Israel wanted a king to reign over them. Against God's warning of what a king would do and be able to claim as his rights, the people of Israel demanded a king. In God's eyes, the people of Israel rejected Him; so, God told Samuel to give them a king. From that time to this very day, there have been governing authorities who have been good and evil, godly and ungodly in their roles. Nevertheless, their *position* of authority has been given by God. Just as they are accountable to God for how they govern, we are accountable to God for obeying the federal, state, and local laws that govern our society. The only exception is when a law requires us to disobey God. As U.S. citizens, we participate in government by voting. Our vote is our voice. While there is no absolutely perfect candidate for office, we must pay attention to decisions made by government officials at every level. We must look beyond the surface and seek to know what they stand for, whether their character is godly or not, whether they stand for the things of God or the things of this world. We have a responsibility to vote conscientiously because the impact of who gets elected will affect our children, grandchildren, great-grandchildren, and generations to come.

Personal Reflection/Application/Prayer: How has God spoken to you through today's WOTD as it relates to your life? How does today's WOTD speak to you/ your situation? What was affirmed? For what do you need to repent? What will you do differently going forward? What commitment to your spiritual growth are you going to make? Is there something that you need from God in order to live His word daily? If not for yourself, for whom do you need to pray as it relates to this WOTD? What can you thank God for and/or declare in confidence according to God's word? What can you boldly and confidently ask God for according to His word? Use the space below to record your personal revelation from God about how these verses apply to you and/or write a personal prayer to God.

day 88

Romans 13:8: **"Owe nothing to anyone—except for your obligation to love one another. If you love your neighbor, you will fulfill the requirements of God's law."** Did you know that you will never be debt-free in this life? Even if you pay off all of your financial obligations, you still have a debt to pay according to Scripture. You owe others unconditional (agape) love. Your neighbor includes strangers, enemies, family, and friends. Your neighbor is whoever is near you at any given moment. The greatest command that we have as Christians is to AGAPE (LOVE): God first, ourselves second, and others third.[55] This agape love is so foundational to who we are that 1 Corinthians 13 says that unless we love others unconditionally, we are nothing and have nothing despite our actions, knowledge, and faith. This love is greater than our faith and hope. This love is who God is and like God, agape lasts forever. To fulfill the requirements of God's law, you must show unconditional love to your neighbor. Read 1 Corinthians 13, paying attention to each characteristic of love. How does it feel to know that you owe EVERYONE this agape? What inner healing must take place for you to be able to agape as God commands you to? Pray about your agape love walk; give those barriers, vulnerabilities, hurts, emotions, etc.… to God; and ask God to help you agape your neighbor like He agapes you.

Personal Reflection/Application/Prayer: How has God spoken to you through today's WOTD as it relates to your life? How does today's WOTD speak to you/your situation? What was affirmed? For what do you need to repent? What will you do differently going forward? What commitment to your spiritual growth are you going to make? Is there something that you need from God in order to live His word daily? If not for yourself, for whom do you need to pray as it relates to this WOTD? What can you thank God for and/or declare in confidence according to God's word? What can you boldly and confidently ask God for according to His word? Use the space below to record your personal revelation from God about how these verses apply to you and/or write a personal prayer to God.

[55] Mark 12:30-31

day 89

Romans 13:9-10: **"For the commandments say, 'You must not commit adultery...murder...steal...covet.' These-and other such commandments-are summed up in this one commandment: 'Love your neighbor as yourself.' Love does no wrong to others, so love fulfills the requirements of God's law."** Our first and greatest command is to love God with everything we have (heart, soul, mind).[56] The second greatest command that God gives us is to love ourselves and love others with the same love that we have for ourselves.[57] The way a person treats others reflects their love for themselves. The actions listed in v. 9 are examples of intentional behaviors that cause hurt and pain to those on the receiving end. No matter how people may try to justify and/or excuse their actions, love is, in no way, at the root of intentional behaviors that wrong others. Think about those whom you have wronged by your actions. What does your treatment of others say about your love for yourself? What will it take for you to apologize to them without trying to excuse your behavior? Take your love issue to God in prayer and ask Him to show you how to love yourself so that you can love others as He commands you to.

Personal Reflection/Application/Prayer: How has God spoken to you through today's WOTD as it relates to your life? How does today's WOTD speak to you/your situation? What was affirmed? For what do you need to repent? What will you do differently going forward? What commitment to your spiritual growth are you going to make? Is there something that you need from God in order to live His word daily? If not for yourself, for whom do you need to pray as it relates to this WOTD? What can you thank God for and/or declare in confidence according to God's word? What can you boldly and confidently ask God for according to His word? Use the space below to record your personal revelation from God about how these verses apply to you and/or write a personal prayer to God.

---

[56] Mark 12:30

[57] Mark 12:31

day 90

Romans 13:11-12: **"This is all the more urgent, for you know how late it is; time is running out. Wake up, for our salvation is nearer now than when we first believed. The night is almost gone; the day of salvation will soon be here. So remove your dark deeds like dirty clothes, and put on the shining armor of right living."** We are truly living in the end times. As my mother used to say, "The Bible is fulfilling" and Jesus is coming back soon. Because we don't know the day nor the hour of Christ's return, it is imperative that we examine ourselves and how we are living now and without delay. My prayer is that God would search all of us and as He finds things that should not be, He will show them to us by His Spirit, including the deception of the devil in our minds that has caused us to embrace wrong thinking and living as right. My prayer is that as God shows us those things that are unpleasing to Him (dark deeds), we will turn from them (remove the dirty clothes) and live as God would have us live according to His word (right living).

Personal Reflection/Application/Prayer: How has God spoken to you through today's WOTD as it relates to your life? How does today's WOTD speak to you/ your situation? What was affirmed? For what do you need to repent? What will you do differently going forward? What commitment to your spiritual growth are you going to make? Is there something that you need from God in order to live His word daily? If not for yourself, for whom do you need to pray as it relates to this WOTD? What can you thank God for and/or declare in confidence according to God's word? What can you boldly and confidently ask God for according to His word? Use the space below to record your personal revelation from God about how these verses apply to you and/or write a personal prayer to God.

day 91

Romans 13:13-14: **"Because we belong to the day, we must live decent lives for all to see. Don't participate in the darkness of wild parties and drunkenness, or in sexual promiscuity and immoral living, or in quarreling and jealousy. Instead, clothe yourself with the presence the Lord Jesus Christ. And don't let yourself think about ways to indulge your evil desires."** There are numerous brands from which to choose when buying the clothes that we wear. Sometimes, companies put their name or symbol on the exterior of their merchandise so that it is evident that you are wearing their brand. Some people are so particular that they will only wear certain brands; anything else is sub-standard to them. Just as we put on clothes in the natural, we also wear spiritual clothes. Whereas there are numerous natural clothing brands, there are only two brands of spiritual clothing: the presence of the Lord Jesus Christ and the presence of satan. How we live our lives reflects our spiritual brand. As children of God, we are to wear the Lord's presence daily. Wearing the presence of the Lord gives us peace about who we are and whose we are; it puts boundaries around our lives to protect us. Wearing the presence of the Lord enables us to use wisdom in our decision-making so that we can live "decent lives for all to see". Wearing the presence of the Lord guards our minds and enables us to see through satan's deception. Satan presents partying, drinking, smoking, sexual immorality of all kinds, etc.... as living the life when it's actually a setup for our destruction. What brand of spiritual clothes does your life reflect? How well do your actions reflect that you belong to Christ? If you know that you have been living as if you belong to darkness in any area of your life, choose at this moment to change your spiritual brand. God loves you so much that He sent Jesus to set you free from darkness. Jesus loves you so much that He shed His blood to give you a new spiritual brand. Accept this love, allow His blood to wash away the darkness, receive His forgiveness, and clothe yourself with His presence. Anything else is sub-standard.

Personal Reflection/Application/Prayer: How has God spoken to you through today's WOTD as it relates to your life? How does today's WOTD speak to you/your situation? What was affirmed? For what do you need to repent? What will you do differently going forward? What commitment to your spiritual growth are you going to make? Is there something that you need from God in order to live His word daily? If not for yourself, for whom do you need to pray as it relates to this WOTD? What can you thank God for and/or declare in confidence according to God's word? What can you boldly and confidently ask God for according to His word? Use the space below to record your personal revelation from God about how these verses apply to you and/or write a personal prayer to God.

day 92

Romans 14:1-6: **"Accept other believers who are weak in faith, and don't argue with them about what they think is right or wrong. For instance, one person believes it's all right to eat anything. But another believer with a sensitive conscience will eat only vegetables. Those who feel free to eat anything must not look down on those who don't. And those who don't eat certain foods must not condemn those who do, for God has accepted them. In the same way, some think one day is more holy than another day, while others think every day is alike. You should each be fully convinced that whichever day you choose is acceptable. Those who worship the Lord on a special day do it to honor him. Those who eat any kind of food do so to honor the Lord, since they give thanks to God before eating. And those who refuse to eat certain foods also want to please the Lord and give thanks to God."** As Christians genuinely believing in and confessing Christ as our Lord and Savior, we're not all at the same place in our faith walk. Some of us are new in the faith; others have been running for Jesus a long time. Some of us have set standards and practices in our lives that we feel help us to be closer to God but are neither required nor prohibited for us as Christians, and that is okay. What's not okay is being critical of those who don't adhere to our select standards and practices, who don't do what we do the way that we do it even though they are not disobeying/dishonoring God. Such differences of opinion over things that God does not require or prohibit are irrelevant and are not to divide us as believers. What matters is our motive behind what we believe and practice as believers. That singular motive is to always honor the Lord. As believers, we need to accept our brothers and sisters in Christ who are weaker in faith than we are in any area of their lives and encourage them to honor the Lord in everything they do as they grow in faith being led by the Holy Spirit, not by man-made standards.

Personal Reflection/Application/Prayer: How has God spoken to you through today's WOTD as it relates to your life? How does today's WOTD speak to you/ your situation? What was affirmed? For what do you need to repent? What will you do differently going forward? What commitment to your spiritual growth are you going to make? Is there something that you need from God in order to live His word daily? If not for yourself, for whom do you need to pray as it relates to this WOTD? What can you thank God for and/or declare in confidence according to God's word? What can you boldly and confidently ask God for according to His word? Use the space below to record your personal revelation from God about how these verses apply to you and/or write a personal prayer to God.

day 93

Romans 14:7-9: **"For we don't live for ourselves or die for ourselves. If we live, it's to honor the Lord. And if we die, it's to honor the Lord. Christ died and rose again for this very purpose—to be Lord both of the living and of the dead."** As believers, the motive behind EVERYTHING that we do should be to honor the Lord whom we serve. This is our reasonable act of worship.[58] We don't have to do everything exactly alike for us to honor the Lord. Resist the temptation to be legalistic like the Pharisees and Sadducees. When you are tempted to look down on or condemn other believers because they are not doing what you think they should do the way you think they should do it, pause; pray; and check yourself. Attempt to understand their reasons. If their reasons are scripturally sound, thank God for giving you understanding. If their reasons aren't scripturally sound, take advantage of the opportunity to rightly divide the word of truth in love so that they will understand God's word and how it applies to their lives.[59] That's called correction and is our responsibility to each other. Remember, condemnation of people is reserved for God alone. Each of us will have to stand before God on Judgment Day and give a personal account for how we lived.

Personal Reflection/Application/Prayer: How has God spoken to you through today's WOTD as it relates to your life? How does today's WOTD speak to you/ your situation? What was affirmed? For what do you need to repent? What will you do differently going forward? What commitment to your spiritual growth are you going to make? Is there something that you need from God in order to live His word daily? If not for yourself, for whom do you need to pray as it relates to this WOTD? What can you thank God for and/or declare in confidence according to God's word? What can you boldly and confidently ask God for according to His word? Use the space below to record your personal revelation from God about how these verses apply to you and/or write a personal prayer to God.

58 Romans 12:1

59 2 Timothy 2:15

day 94

Romans 14:17-19: **"For the Kingdom of God is not a matter of what we eat or drink, but of living a life of goodness and peace and joy in the Holy Spirit. If you serve Christ with this attitude, you will please God, and others will approve of you, too. So then, let us aim for harmony in the church and try to build each other up."** If you base the depth of your faith on how strictly you adhere to rules, you're in religion – not relationship. This is dangerous because you can cause other believers to stumble in their relationship with God. Truly living in the Kingdom of God is not about legalism/rule-following. It is about depending on the Holy Spirit, who enables us to live a life of goodness, peace, and joy in harmony with other believers. It enables us to build up our brothers and sisters in Christ. This, not how well we follow rules, pleases God. When other believers see us living authentically in this way, they will approve of us too, and the body of Christ will be strengthened.

Personal Reflection/Application/Prayer: How has God spoken to you through today's WOTD as it relates to your life? How does today's WOTD speak to you/ your situation? What was affirmed? For what do you need to repent? What will you do differently going forward? What commitment to your spiritual growth are you going to make? Is there something that you need from God in order to live His word daily? If not for yourself, for whom do you need to pray as it relates to this WOTD? What can you thank God for and/or declare in confidence according to God's word? What can you boldly and confidently ask God for according to His word? Use the space below to record your personal revelation from God about how these verses apply to you and/or write a personal prayer to God.

day 95

Romans 14:20, 22-23: **"Don't tear apart the work of God over what you eat. Remember, all foods are acceptable, but it is wrong to eat something if it makes another person stumble...You may believe there's nothing wrong with what you are doing, but keep it between yourself and God. Blessed are those who don't feel guilty for doing something they have decided is right. But if you have doubts about whether or not you should eat something, you are sinning if you go ahead and do it. For you are not following your convictions. If you do anything you believe is not right, you are sinning."** There are behaviors that God's word has explicitly told us are wrong, sinful for us to do: worshiping other gods, murder, sexual immorality, etc. There are other behaviors that God has not explicitly forbidden. These verses address the latter. Paul used food, for which the Jews had strict regulations, as an example to teach an important principle. The word of God clearly teaches that God has made all food clean for us to eat. The Jews who continued to follow the Jewish regulations for which food they ate were not wrong for doing so if they felt that doing so helped them to honor God. Likewise, those who didn't follow the Jewish food regulations were not wrong for not doing so if they felt that they were honoring God. The issue here is one of personal conviction about sin in our decisions, which is the principle we must apply to our lives. If you are unsure as to whether you should do something, you shouldn't do it because doing it causes you to sin as far as God is concerned. Whenever you go against your convictions, you are sinning as far as God is concerned. When God shows you that something is wrong for you, don't do it regardless of who is doing it. (Pork is perfectly fine to eat; however, it is wrong for you to eat it if eating it causes your blood pressure to go up.) To pressure someone into doing something they are unsure of puts a stumbling block in their way. One example of this is in the church is using wine for Communion. For a recovering alcoholic, this presents a stumbling block. Even the smell of wine could cause someone to fail in their sobriety. If you're as honest with yourself and I was with myself when the Holy Spirit gave me understanding of these verses, you'll agree that this is a good place to pause, pray, and repent for either going against your convictions at some point in your life and/or putting a stumbling block in someone's path because of expectations you put on them. If you've never done this, don't start doing it.

Personal Reflection/Application/Prayer: How has God spoken to you through today's WOTD as it relates to your life? How does today's WOTD speak to you/ your situation? What was affirmed? For what do you need to repent? What will you do differently going forward? What commitment to your spiritual growth are you going to make? Is there something that you need from God in order to live His word daily? If not for yourself, for whom do you need to pray as it relates to this WOTD? What can you thank God for and/or declare in confidence according to God's word? What can you boldly and confidently ask God for according to His word? Use the space below to record your personal revelation from God about how these verses apply to you and/or write a personal prayer to God.

day 96

Romans 15:1-3a: **"We who are strong must be considerate of those who are sensitive about things like this. We must not just please ourselves. We should help others do what is right and build them up in the Lord. For even Christ didn't live to please himself."** There isn't room for selfishness in the body of Christ. Those of us who are strong in our faith have a responsibility to build up those who aren't yet strong, to seek to understand their sensitivities rather than press our preferences upon them. We aren't to take advantage of what they don't yet know or understand; rather, we are to help them do what is right in the Lord's eyes. We are to help them live in love, truth, peace, and integrity according to God's word. Be intentional today about encouraging other believers in their faith.

Personal Reflection/Application/Prayer: How has God spoken to you through today's WOTD as it relates to your life? How does today's WOTD speak to you/ your situation? What was affirmed? For what do you need to repent? What will you do differently going forward? What commitment to your spiritual growth are you going to make? Is there something that you need from God in order to live His word daily? If not for yourself, for whom do you need to pray as it relates to this WOTD? What can you thank God for and/or declare in confidence according to God's word? What can you boldly and confidently ask God for according to His word? Use the space below to record your personal revelation from God about how these verses apply to you and/or write a personal prayer to God.

day 97

Romans 15:7-9a: **"Therefore, accept each other just as Christ has accepted you so that God will be given glory. Remember that Christ came as a servant to the Jews to show that God is true to the promises he made to their ancestors. He also came so that the Gentiles might give glory to God for his mercies to them."** Despite Jesus coming to both Jews and Gentiles to unify the church, there was division among them. The body of Christ is not called to merely tolerate or put up with each other. There should be no clicks or discrimination within the church. The call to accept each other just as Christ has accepted us is a call to remember how Jesus accepted us despite our sins, flaws, and background. It is a call to extend the same love, grace, and mercy to other believers that Christ extended to us. It is a call to share in each other's lives more than just when we come together for a service or event. How accepting are you of other believers who don't look like or do things exactly like you? Do you offer conditional acceptance? Do you extend yourself to believers outside of those with whom you are comfortable? Is God glorified by how you treat ALL of your brothers and sisters in Christ? How accepting is your church of ALL believers? Is God glorified by how your church treats ALL believers? Imagine how your church would be transformed if every member was accepted in this way. Imagine how the church - the body of Christ at-large - could transform our communities if we accepted each other in this way. How can you be more personally accepting of ALL believers? How can your church glorify God by accepting ALL believers?

Personal Reflection/Application/Prayer: How has God spoken to you through today's WOTD as it relates to your life? How does today's WOTD speak to you/your situation? What was affirmed? For what do you need to repent? What will you do differently going forward? What commitment to your spiritual growth are you going to make? Is there something that you need from God in order to live His word daily? If not for yourself, for whom do you need to pray as it relates to this WOTD? What can you thank God for and/or declare in confidence according to God's word? What can you boldly and confidently ask God for according to His word? Use the space below to record your personal revelation from God about how these verses apply to you and/or write a personal prayer to God.

day 98

Romans 16:17-18: **"And now I make one more appeal, my dear brothers and sisters. Watch out for people who cause divisions and upset people's faith by teaching things contrary to what you have been taught. Stay away from them. Such people are not serving Christ our Lord; they are serving their own personal interests. By smooth talk and glowing words they deceive innocent people."** The first smooth talker who intentionally used words to captivate and deceive his innocent listener was satan disguised as a serpent in Genesis 3. Today, he speaks his lies through people who pretend to serve the Lord, who claim that there are ways to God other than through Christ, who teach that the Holy Spirit is not real, who deny that Jesus and God are one, who teach that you are God because you were created in His image, and who teach all manner of things contrary to the word of God. Don't entertain the company of these people or listen to their message. They are wolves in sheep's clothing. Whether they realize it or not, these people are on assignment by satan to pervert God's word and lead people away from Christ. They prey on your lack of knowledge and understanding of God's word. They prey on your weaknesses, listening as you unknowingly reveal them, and saying the very things that appeal to those vulnerabilities. They show up consistently, waiting for you to take the bait and act on the lies they put on their hook. Today, more than ever, it is important for EVERY CHRISTIAN to get in God's word. God's word is truth; it is your sword of attack against false teaching. Study God's word to show yourself approved so that you will not be ashamed and can rightly divide the word of truth.[60] It will enable you to distinguish between God's truth and the enemy's lies, which are aimed at your destruction.

Personal Reflection/Application/Prayer: How has God spoken to you through today's WOTD as it relates to your life? How does today's WOTD speak to you/ your situation? What was affirmed? For what do you need to repent? What will you do differently going forward? What commitment to your spiritual growth are you going to make? Is there something that you need from God in order to live His

[60] 2 Timothy 2:15

word daily? If not for yourself, for whom do you need to pray as it relates to this WOTD? What can you thank God for and/or declare in confidence according to God's word? What can you boldly and confidently ask God for according to His word? Use the space below to record your personal revelation from God about how these verses apply to you and/or write a personal prayer to God.

Dear Reader,

I hope and pray that you have benefited from our walk through Romans. I shared with you the insights and spiritual nuggets that I received from the Holy Spirit through my study and meditation on God's word. As you have read, meditated on, and prayed about how each WOTD applies to your life, I believe that the Holy Spirit has given you insight and spiritual nuggets that you can share with others to help build them up in their Christian faith.

If you have benefited from taking this journey with me through Romans, I would love to hear from you directly about how:

- God spoke to you (direction, correction, affirmation, etc.);
- Your relationship with Christ has been strengthened; and
- The Holy Spirit gave you revelation that sparked transformation in your life as a Christian. Please email me at wotd4me@gmail.com.

May God continue to grow you through His word and may your light shine brighter in your spheres of influence because you took the time to invest in your spiritual growth through the WORD OF THE DAY.

Rev. Sherol

Printed in the United States
by Baker & Taylor Publisher Services